Forty Plus

For many men and women midlife is a time of unprecedented change. There is physical change. There are changes at home — teenagers growing up, parents growing old. There are changes at work — for some the drastic change of redundancy or early retirement. Each fresh situation brings its own challenge and its own losses.

The trouble with midlife is that the losses often seem to outweigh the gains. But it does not have to be like that. For those who are prepared to take stock, midlife can be positive and exciting, offering new directions and a fresh start.

Having come through her own difficult midlife period, Mary Batchelor draws on personal experience, and draws widely on the experience of others, to provide help and information, and sympathetic understanding.

She offers practical advice on health and beauty, at the same time suggesting that there is an inner beauty which need not fade as we grow older. Difficulties are faced honestly. Are we prepared to deal with the past, to let go the 'if onlys' and the bitterness of hurt? Without this we will be unable to move forward into full enjoyment of both middle and old age.

Midlife provides the opportunity to look again at who we are, at priorities and values, and at where we are going. Then we can face the future with faith and the confident hope of increasing enrichment of life — to the end.

FORTY PLUS

MARY BATCHELOR

A LION PAPERBACK
Tring • Batavia • Sydney

Published by
Lion Publishing plc
Icknield Way, Tring, Herts, England
ISBN 0 7459 1363 6
Albatross Books Pty Ltd
PO Box 320, Sutherland, NSW 2232, Australia
ISBN 0 86760 989 3

First edition 1988

British Library Cataloguing in Publication Data
Batchelor, Mary
  Forty plus
1. Middle age. Personal adjustment
I. Title
305.2'44

ISBN 0-7459-1363-6

Printed and bound in Great Britain
by Cox and Wyman Ltd, Reading

CONTENTS

SECTION 6: THE WORLD OF WORK

SECTION 7: PROFIT AND LOSS

AUTHOR'S PREFACE

Much of the material in this book has been supplied by real people — at midlife, or beyond — who have generously shared their experiences with me. In some cases we had not met before and I very much appreciate the willingness of these new-made friends who shared private and personal experiences with me, in order to help others. My friends and family also contributed and so did many others, whose chance comments or strongly felt views were added to the sum of my findings about the years from forty onwards. In every case, names and a few minor details have been altered to spare them the embarrassment of being recognized. Since they will remain unknown, I am all the more anxious to take this opportunity of thanking them from my heart for all the help that they gave.

I am also deeply grateful to the many professional people who shared their hard-won expertise and wisdom with me. General practitioners, psychotherapists, counsellors, social workers, as well as many others with specialist knowledge, generously spared their time and shared their insights with me. I am most grateful to them all. A group of marriage guidance counsellors gave up a lunch hour to pool their ideas and experiences. Personnel and counsellors from CRUSE, Stepfamilies, National Council for Carers and The Children's Society also gave me a great deal of time and valuable information. As always, the staff of the local library were unfailingly helpful and patient, tracing and providing some of the books that I needed.

It has not been possible to cover all situations in a book of this scope. There is no special information, for example, to help those with disabled teenagers, or those in midlife coping with disablement themselves. On the other hand, no one person is likely to need all the information covered in the various sections of the book. I hope, nonetheless, that the varied needs and situations of midlife have been broadly covered. Any chapters that are not relevant can be skipped, or read in order to enter more imaginatively into the situations of those who are facing experiences different from our own.

INTRODUCTION

Most of us relish the idea of a change. We often feel tired and stale, and imprisoned by the monotony of everyday life. We scan brochures and plan next year's vacation with enthusiasm. But the break with routine that a holiday brings lasts for only a few weeks, and we probably enjoy the change all the more because we know that the old familiar things are waiting for us at the end of the journey home.

Holidays apart, the real changes in life usually mark the beginning of new circumstances and new situations. They involve the permanent loss of old and familiar ways. What hits us, sometimes with relief, but more often with sadness or anxiety, is the fact that life will never be the same again.

Change is sometimes dramatic and sudden — the start of a new job, new home or new marriage. More often it creeps up on us unawares, and the effects are so gradual that we only take notice when something draws our attention to the altered state of affairs that has overtaken us.

Change of one kind or another characterizes the whole of life, but some stages are more obviously disrupted by change than others. Adolescence is the most obvious example, and midlife comes a close second.

Midlife is a difficult period to pin down precisely. How and when it occurs can vary widely. Some people at thirty-five have children in their teens and are already preparing for the time when their sons and daughters will leave home. Other couples are embarking on their first — or last — baby at forty, and would still consider themselves more akin to the younger generation. It is impossible to give hard and fast age limits, but most people reach midlife roughly between the ages of forty and fifty-five.

This middle stage of life is often referred to as 'midlife crisis' — a dramatic-sounding label which is enough to dismay anyone approaching thirty-five. 'Crisis' conjures up visions of near desperation and a moment in time when all the simmering undercurrents of increasing worry and pressure come to the boil. Our everyday use of the word encourages us to think along those lines but the original meaning is rather different.

'Crisis' was used at first to define the point in an illness when the patient took a turn, either for the better or for the worse. Before the discovery of antibiotics, a doctor or nurse would sit at the bedside of a patient suffering, for example, from pneumonia, waiting helplessly until the crisis arrived. At that turning-point the patient would either fall into a health-giving sleep or sink into unconsciousness and death.

By this definition midlife crisis means the turning-point which occurs at midlife in the lives of most of us. How that turning-point is handled is going to affect the rest of our lives. It is possible to progress into a healthy and stimulating second half of life or, for those unable to come to terms with changed conditions and circumstances, to withdraw from growth and real living and opt for security and 'safe' non-participation.

Differences of sex, occupation, and temperament have a bearing on how we experience midlife. Some are propelled into change as the direct result of some shattering life event such as death, divorce or redundancy. Others tackle gradual changes as they occur and make readjustments to their thinking and lifestyle over several months or even years. There are as many variables as there are people. Here are some people reaching midlife crisis in very different ways.

Jonathan has been made redundant after thirty years with the same firm. At forty-eight he is finding difficulty in getting another job. He feels a failure in comparison with his wife, who works full-time. She expects him to be grateful that she is earning and to do his bit by seeing to the housework and shopping. Jonathan is not yet able to cope with the role change or the feelings of inadequacy which he is experiencing.

Olive is fifty-four and unmarried. She holds a senior position in banking. Her mother, who lives with her, is becoming increasingly incapable because of senile dementia. It is important for Olive to work, both for her own well-being and for the pension she will get on retirement, but the strain of coping with her mother and holding down a top-level job is becoming increasingly heavy.

At forty, Janet is struggling with a marriage that involves sharing the role of grandmother with her second husband's former wife, caring for her husband's bachelor son, who is suffering from depression, and agonizing over her own teenage children who are living with their father and his girlfriend. She is working part-time to help family finances and suffering from guilt, exhaustion and anxiety about the success of her second marriage.

Pamela is forty-five and admits that she has everything. She is ashamed of feeling deeply unhappy in spite of her lovely home and garden, stable marriage and absence of anything to worry about. But her three daughters have left home, her husband is immersed in work and spends very little time at home and the future seems to stretch ahead of her like a barren desert.

At forty, Melvin is utterly bored and frustrated by a dead-end job. He believes that he has the ability to make a success of a small business of his own. He has looked into the possibility of getting a loan and setting up the whole operation. But his wife is unwilling to take the risk and criticizes him for being dissatisfied and throwing up a good job with a pension to come at sixty-five. Melvin's secretary, on the other hand, admires his initiative and would be ready to leave her job and join him in the new venture.

All these very different men and women are facing their own midlife crises. They are experiencing the tensions, challenges and losses which characterize this period in life. At this stage the losses may appear to outweigh the gains. Most men are conscious that they can no longer beat the youngsters in any and every display of physical strength or speed. Most women take a look in the mirror and realize that they no longer look young, or as sexually attractive as their daughters or nieces or the youngster down the road. The fact that there are other kinds of strengths or good looks than those of youth may not, at this stage, bring much comfort.

There are losses brought about by outward events too. Parents who have been the carers and supporters begin to need care and support themselves. Those with families face what is often called the 'empty nest syndrome'. There may be the loss of one or other partner in marriage, through death or desertion. For women, the menopause brings the realization that childbearing years are over. Last, but by no means least, there is the strong possibility in our society of redundancy or enforced early retirement, sometimes with little possibility of further employment.

The combination of personal, inward change and the external events that trigger change often create the same kind of questions and doubts in the mind that characterize the teen-age years. People in midlife are shocked to find that they are wrestling with problems and queries that they imagined they had settled long ago, once and for all:

'Who am I and what am I doing that is of any value?'

'What has my life amounted to so far?'

'Is this all there is to life?'

'Have I any kind of future or do I face nothing but old age and death?'

Normally sensible and competent people, who have previously got on more or less happily with the business of living, find themselves stopped in their tracks by questions like these. Just as teenagers need to find out who they are and where they are going before they are ready to embark on adult life, so most of us facing what has been called 'second adolescence' need to discover our real identity and set ourselves new goals. The aims and aspirations of our twenties and thirties are no longer appropriate to the forties and fifties and will certainly not satisfy us for the rest of life.

Sometimes people are unwilling to admit to the crisis that they are facing. Bishop Jim Thompson, in his book *Half Way*, comments: 'Many of us men are confused but it's not part of the male role to admit it.' Men, he goes on to suggest, feel about midlife as they do about religion, that it is something best left to women. But if the crisis is an important turning-point, then it is necessary to be aware of what is happening in order to take up the right options.

Some of the choices will be practical ones, concerned with work and family, but the most important decisions are the deeper ones which reflect the personal attitudes and priorities that motivate our behaviour. In these areas the passage from the old to the new may not always be smooth and easy. Midlife is uncomfortable because it often leaves us stranded for a time in a no-man's-land between one phase of life and the next. This transition stage may last for months or even a few years.

Gail Sheehy, in her book *Passages*, uses the picture of changing chairs: 'We must be willing to change chairs if we want to grow. There is no permanent compatibility between a chair and a person. And there is no one right chair. What is right at one stage may be too restricting at another or too soft. During the passage from one stage to another we will be between two chairs. Wobbling, no doubt, but developing. . . Times of crisis, or disruption or constructive change, are not only predictable but desirable. They mean growth.'

In this book we aim to look at some of the major and minor changes that occur during the middle years. These include physical and physiological changes, the most significant of which is the menopause. There are suggestions for keeping healthy and retaining a sense of well-being and confidence appropriate to the new age-range. Emotional and spiritual needs are considered, as well as the new situations that often arise at work, at home and in the family.

A book dealing with this period of life may appear to include a good number of problems, but that is inevitable. It is reassuring to remember that some people sail through midlife with few if any problems, and most experience only a few of those listed. I have tried to strike the balance between an unrealistic optimism about this stage of life — which can be infuriating and distressing to anyone searching for help — and a pessimistic recital of all possible ills and problems.

When I was coping with midlife I would have liked to find a book that reassured me that there was nothing abnormal in what I was experiencing and that offered me practical help and advice. I should also have found it helpful to know what other people might be experiencing, in order to understand them better. This book is intended as that kind of resource.

The overall approach to the subject is intended to be positive and optimistic. I have emerged myself from a difficult midlife crisis. There was a time when it seemed as if every event of importance and value lay in the past — that life from now on would be downhill all the way. Yet I have now discovered a richness and quality of life which I never knew before. My own experience is that the second half of life is better than the first. What seemed at one time to be a permanent sense of discomfort and uprooting was the preliminary to a new and more stimulating quality of living.

Best of all, I can confirm from personal experience that God is ready to be involved with men and women at every stage of life. He gave me the courage and strength I needed, even when I did not feel as though he was close. My own Christian faith has not made pain or loss or difficulty any less, but it has helped me to face circumstances honestly, to find purpose in life as it really is, and to have the certain knowledge that God is with me in it all. That confidence will last for the rest of life and beyond, and it is available to everyone.

SECTION 1
THE CHANGE

1
THE MENOPAUSE

The Things People Say

'I have had a lot of trouble in my time, and most of it never happened.'
Elderly woman, quoted by Joan Malleson in *Change of Life*

'Hardly any physiological change is the subject of so much speculation and morbid fantasy as is the menopause today.'
Dr Brice Pitt in *Making the Most of Middle Age*

'It's not realistic to think of the menopause as a big bogey but it is important to acknowledge that there will be changes. Go half way — don't be alarmed but don't pooh pooh it.'
Psychiatrist and therapist

'It's the individual's ability to cope with menopause symptoms that matters. Someone like a headmistress might need treatment because of the demands of her job, whereas another woman with the same objective level of malfunction might cope because her job was less tense.'
Woman doctor

'There's no doubt that the fuller your life is and the more active you are, the less you will be bothered with the menopause.'
Dr Jean Coope in *The Menopause*

'If a person becomes preoccupied with a symptom she needs treatment — not because of how severe it is but because it is disabling to her.' Woman doctor

'I got the impression that you'd got to get through hot flushes so I thought if that's the case, let's get on with it. I never went to the doctor at all. I just told myself, "You'll grow out of it one of these days."'
Older woman

'Forget the old wives' tales about "the Change" marking the beginning of the end — and think positive.'
Maryon Stewart, Women's Nutritional Advisory Service,
writing in *Home and Freezer*

'HRT keeps women out of the orthopaedic wards, mad house and the divorce courts.'
John Studd, consultant gynaecologist

Once upon a time, the verdict on any woman between the ages of forty and fifty, suffering from one of any number of different ills, would be, 'It's the change!' The words were usually spoken in a conspiratorial whisper which added to the mystique surrounding the whole terrible ordeal. Nowadays the menopause is discussed freely and openly and most magazine articles favour the same approach as many doctors — a brisk, no-nonsense treatment of the subject as a perfectly normal and usually uneventful process in every woman's life.

The truth probably lies somewhere between the two extremes, with the emphasis on the modern view. The good news is that many women do indeed experience little more than minor discomforts during the menopause and a few suffer none at all. For those who do have unpleasant side effects there is medical help to be had.

But, in spite of what a cheery doctor may say, many women complain of somehow not feeling themselves and recognize that they are reacting to life in uncharacteristic ways. Worse still, other members of the family don't hesitate to tell them the same thing. All kinds of aches and pains seem to add to the difficulties at this time, but since these are often years of extra pressures at home and at work it is not surprising if some symptoms of stress occur anyway, irrespective of the menopause. One doctor pointed out that stress can, in itself, cause hormonal changes, so outward events as well as glandular imbalance may be to blame.

The menopause is often held responsible for a whole range of ills. Dr Brice Pitt comments in his book *Making the Most of Middle Age*, 'Any doctor knows that his female patients are liable to blame the change for any disorder or mishap which may befall them from their early thirties onwards. And, in all honesty, he may not know whether they are right or not, or what he can do about it anyway!'

What exactly is the menopause?

Literally, the word menopause means the end of a woman's monthly periods and therefore signifies the end of the time in her life in which she is able to have children. But the word is more often used in a general way to cover the whole process of body change which may begin three or more years before periods stop and continue for several more years afterwards. From the menarche (start of periods) a woman's body produces an egg every month, which is capable of being fertilized. If it is not fertilized, the egg is expelled from the body along with the specially prepared womb lining and the extra supply of blood which has been provided to nourish a fertilized egg. This discharge of blood and lining occurs as the monthly period. When a woman reaches midlife, the body begins to cut down on its production of oestrogen, the hormone which triggers ovulation. The womb no longer prepares for fertilization, so periods stop. Hormone levels may vary over a length of time, so the process may take several years before it is completed.

When will it happen?

Just as the start of periods varies from one person to another, so there is no fixed age at which the menopause will take place. Most doctors are sceptical of women who begin to blame 'the change' for how they feel at forty but a few (very few) do begin as early as that, while at the other extreme some women may continue with periods until the age of fifty-three or four. The commonest age is round about fifty.

Most medical experts dismiss the notion of any link between the age at which a woman begins periods and that at which she stops — in other words, she won't stop early because she began early or go on longer if she was a late starter. She may follow a similar pattern to her mother's but even that is by no means certain. Doctors do recommend that any woman still having periods after fifty-five should go to her doctor for advice.

It is reassuring to know that a woman who has suffered every month from pre-menstrual tension is not necessarily going to have problems with mood swings and tension when the menopause affects her hormone balance.

How will it happen?

There are various ways in which any particular woman may experience the end of periods. It may be:

• **Gradual** This is probably the most usual way. Periods become more and more scanty and finally stop altogether, or the gap between periods becomes greater until they stop. Sometimes a very heavy period may be followed by none for a few months and the process repeated. The fact that things are irregular may cause inconvenience and even embarrassment to a woman who has always had a very regular pattern of periods but at least it is a welcome sign that the beginning of the end has arrived.

• **Sudden** Some women may stop periods abruptly, once and for all. Anne was fifty-four when her elderly mother died. Her periods stopped from that day. Miriam was about forty-eight when her husband was taken desperately ill and not expected to survive. He did — but her periods stopped then. Other women may find that, although some sudden bout of stress stops periods temporarily, they begin again for a time when the crisis is over.

• **Artificial** Artificial menopause is the term used when periods end as a result of a hysterectomy, or removal of the womb by surgery. More about that later.

Some women may be disconcerted to find that, instead of fewer periods, they are having heavier and more frequent ones. They may last for two or three weeks with barely a month between them. Allowing for the fact that a woman often believes that she is losing more blood than she actually is, it is still possible to become anaemic and it is important to go to the doctor and tell him or her if this is happening.

It is a good idea to keep a note of when you have a period and how heavy or light it is. If you have to see the doctor he is almost certain to question you about dates.

Most women do not want to become pregnant at this stage so it is important to continue using contraception even when periods seem to have stopped. It is safe to assume that periods have stopped altogether only after one full year without a period for a woman over fifty and two full years for those under fifty. Hormone Replacement Therapy (HRT) does not act as a contraceptive.

What are the symptoms of the menopause?

The symptoms recognized by doctors certainly do not cover the full range of complaints that many women cite as part of the menopause. But there are one or two symptoms which every doctor is willing to attribute to the change. The one most talked about and most commonly experienced by women is the hot flush (or flash). About eighty per cent of women suffer from them at some stage, although they are far less of a nuisance for some than for others. A hot flush consists of a sudden feeling of warmth, mainly in the face and neck and upper part of the body. For many women the chief problem is their own acute embarrassment. They feel sure that everyone in the room can see what is happening, but few people are that observant and, anyway, if there is a mirror nearby, a quick glance in it will often reveal no more than a becoming blush!

But the flush can be more troublesome if it is accompanied by profuse sweating. Sometimes too there are palpitations which have nothing at all to do with any heart disorder but can be uncomfortable and a little frightening at first. Hot flushes can be a nuisance at night. A wife who is constantly throwing back the bedclothes may disturb her husband as well and, if it becomes necessary to keep changing a nightdress wet with sweat, a good night's sleep may be impossible.

It is important to realize that very few women find hot flushes as troublesome as this. If they do, they should go to the doctor. He or she can prescribe Hormone Replacement Therapy which deals most effectively with the trouble. Hot flushes may begin before periods stop but they mainly occur in the two or three years following and, for a few women, may continue off and on even longer. An eighty-five-year-old neighbour told me that she had a trouble-free menopause, but still suffers from hot flushes!

Many women dread hot flushes long before they experience them but it's important to realize that twenty per cent of women never have a single one and for many others they are nothing more than a minor nuisance and certainly won't continue for ever. So it is worth being philosophical about the whole matter, knowing that should they become bad enough to make life a misery, medical help is available. Meanwhile, it is best to try not to take it all too seriously or to dread the feeling that heralds a flush.

One friend has warned her work colleagues — men and women — to take no notice when she begins to strip off. Most of us would not go as far as that, but it is important to keep the whole matter in proportion and to worry less.

One reassuring fact about hot flushes is that they have nothing at all to do with heightened blood pressure. On the other hand, they do not seem to have any particular value and are not 'worth a guinea a time', as our grandmothers used to affirm.

A few tips can make hot flushes more manageable:

• Wear several layers of light clothing, so that some can easily be removed — and replaced afterwards!

• Avoid polo and high-necked styles

• Wear cotton, not man-made fibres, for bra and underwear.

• Take tepid showers.

• Avoid alcohol and coffee.

Another effect of the slow-down of oestrogen production is a drying of the vagina, which may make sex painful. A lubricating jelly may help. (K-Y and other proprietary brands can be bought over the counter.) But the doctor can prescribe hormone cream or hormone tablets which will put the condition right. (NB Hormone cream should not be used just before intercourse because of adverse effects on your partner.) The changed condition of the vagina can also mean an added tendency to develop infections such as thrush or cystitis. There may be burning or itching or vaginal discharge. Any of these problems should be reported to the doctor.

Doctors are often sceptical about other complaints that are attributed to the menopause and judging from the number of suggested symptoms, they are probably right to put many of them down to old wives' tales. From a variety of sources, I have compiled the following list of complaints associated, by non-medical people at least, with the menopause:

• hot flushes

• dizziness

• lack of concentration

• panic attacks

• loss of confidence

• rheumatic pains

• decreased sex drive

• palpitations

• dry vagina

• night sweats

• headaches

• moodiness

• irritability

• sweating

• weight increase

• backache

• insomnia

• anxiety

- painful intercourse
- facial hair
- confusedness
- tiredness
- water retention

- constipation
- depression
- insomnia
- nervousness
- general malaise

It seems highly unlikely that all these symptoms can really be blamed on the menopause, but there is no doubt that some women suffer a number of minor ailments which make the daily routine a burden. Hormone Replacement Therapy (HRT), prescribed for hormone deficiency, does sometimes clear up a number of other symptoms and improve the health overall. But HRT is not a magic pill or a cure-all and, in any case, much will depend on your own doctor's attitude as to whether they are willing to prescribe it.

When to consult a doctor

Most women are far too busy to go to the doctor unless it is really necessary and would rather soldier on without medical advice. Dr Jean Coope, in her book, *Menopause*, suggests that it is common sense to have a routine medical check-up around the time of the menopause. The check would include height, weight and blood pressure measurement, examination of breasts and pelvis, a urine test, a cervical smear test and a discussion of any problems bothering you.

Some may doubt if their doctor would welcome the request for such a time-consuming check of a well person, but it could be worth trying. Sometimes it is important to see a doctor to make sure that all is well: this is not fussing or taking up their time unnecessarily. It is also worth setting your own mind at rest if you are worried about any symptoms. You should certainly see the doctor if:

- periods are so heavy that it means going to bed, or if they last so long that there are very few free days between them.

- there is irregular bleeding, that is, if you have a show of blood between periods or after intercourse.

- periods are very painful.

- hot flushes make normal life difficult or disturb nights severely.

- a hot, dry vagina makes intercourse painful.

NB Before you visit the doctor, check on your chart marking dates of periods over the last months, note any other details and take the information with you.

Don't worry!
Some women have particular health worries during the menopause. Blood pressure is less of a problem for women than for men before this age, but it can occur at midlife. If you have any worries on this score, a check by the doctor will take only a couple of minutes and will set your mind at rest.

Bleeding that is heavy or that occurs at an unexpected time can be frightening. Without mentioning the word, many women jump to the conclusion that they might have cancer, which they believe is common at this age. The main reason why cancer is associated with the menopause is that irregular bleeding can more easily be overlooked or not reported during this time. There is every chance that the fears are unfounded but it is important to report irregular bleeding so that, in the unlikely event of cancer being present, early treatment can be given. A cure is even more certain when cancer is diagnosed and treated early.

Another cause of heavy bleeding is fibroids. These are non-malignant lumps of muscle in the wall of the womb that may need to be removed by surgery. Painful periods at this or any other time may be caused by fibroids and also by endometriosis. This is a condition where the endometrium, the tissue which lines the womb, begins to grow in other parts of the lower body, causing pain and extra bleeding. It may be possible to treat mild cases with drugs, otherwise by hysterectomy.

Long-term effects of oestrogen loss
One of the long-term effects of loss of oestrogen in the body, which occurs at the menopause, is the gradual thinning of the bones. This is the reason why older women are more liable to suffer fractures. Sometimes osteoporosis causes some curving of the spine in middle-aged women, rather unkindly referred to as 'dowager's hump'. Doctors now think that even two to three years on HRT slows down bone-thinning to a great extent and those who favour hormone replacement add this 'plus' to

their reasons for prescribing it. Osteoporosis has become quite a talking-point recently and the emphasis has been put on prevention by natural means, which includes exercise and a diet which contains plenty of calcium.

Hormone Replacement Therapy (HRT)

Hormone replacement began to take off in the United States in 1966 through the efforts of a British-born doctor, Robert Wilson, who equated the restoring of hormone balance with the restoring of a woman's femininity. Oestrogen became popular not only to counteract the medical effects of the menopause but also to keep women youthful in body and mind. Then came fears, well-founded, that prolonged doses of oestrogen could result in far greater incidence of cancer of the womb. The answer is to change to a combined oestrogen and progesterone treatment. The hormones are usually given in tablet form for three weeks at a time. During the fourth week bleeding similar to a period occurs. This form of HRT seems to be very safe, although from time to time results of tests seem to show possible side effects, such as breast cancer. So HRT is not given lightly or without due regard to a woman's medical history and most women on HRT are given a cervical smear and a womb scrape every two or three years, in case the bleeding which might signify early cancer has been masked by the HRT.

As things are at present, only about two per cent of women receive HRT in Britain. In the United States figures are much higher — more like thirty per cent. It has been estimated that two thirds of British doctors are still sceptical about the value of the treatment, although there are now special clinics in some large cities dealing specifically with menopause problems and hormone treatment. It is sometimes possible to attend such a clinic without referral from your doctor.

Most of us would prefer to use natural methods to cope with the menopause. For example, the British-based Women's Nutritional Advisory Service lays emphasis on the importance of a healthy diet to overcome many of the problems. In addition, vitamin E is recommended to alleviate hot flushes, headaches and vaginal troubles, evening primrose oil to relieve stress and zinc to regulate hormone changes. Some women may find a multi-vitamin and mineral preparation helpful, but it is always wise to ask a doctor's advice before taking other extra vitamins. Dosing yourself can be harmful.

Hysterectomy

Suzie Hayman, in her book *Hysterectomy*, quotes the experience of one woman, who said, 'By the time I saw my doctor I knew that there was something seriously wrong and that my womb would have to go. I can't describe the feelings of horror, of desolation almost that hit me when he said, "It'll have to come out, Mrs B." What was so awful was that he quite obviously thought I was silly to feel upset. I'd had my family . . . I couldn't explain that it was me — the centre of my whole life — that he was wanting to slice out and throw away.'

Not every woman reacts so strongly to the idea of a hysterectomy, but many do feel very differently about having their womb removed from how they would about having tonsils or appendix taken out. Some women believe, consciously or unconsciously, that it is the ability to have children that makes them feminine. They think that without a womb they would be less than a complete woman. Not all doctors understand such a reaction to what they think of as a perfectly routine operation.

Many myths that surround the subject also need exploding. It is just not true that 'You'll never be the same again' or 'Sex is over for you' or 'You'll be less of a woman'. Even the traditional idea that it takes six months to get over the operation is exaggerated and so is the belief that depression will naturally follow. Getting fat is not a necessary consequence of the operation either. Weight increase is more likely to be the result of less exercise combined with extra 'treats'.

The right way to deal with the fears and misunderstandings that surround hysterectomy is to bring them out into the open and find reassurance before the time comes to go into hospital. Both partners in a marriage need counselling to allay their fears. It will help them to learn about the positive benefits to the wife's health which the operation will bring, as well as the potential for full sexual enjoyment by both partners after the operation is over.

There are two ways of performing a hysterectomy, one through the vagina, leaving no scar, and the other through a small incision which can often be below the bikini line. If both the womb and ovaries have to be removed — which is by no means always the case — there will be a sudden loss of oestrogen, so hormone implants are usually given to prevent hot flushes and other side effects that could otherwise follow.

There are several helpful books specifically about hysterectomy giving all the information that could be wished for, including what to take into hospital, what to expect before and after the operation, as well as what is actually being done at the time. Those having the operation might also like to check whether there is a hysterectomy support group in the area. If not, why not start one?

ACTION CHECKPOINTS

☐ Keep your menopause in proportion — don't worry!

☐ Fill your mind and time with plenty of other interests.

☐ Treat yourself kindly — don't take on extra work.

☐ Get some rest each day.

☐ Check with doctor about any abnormal bleeding or symptoms that make normal living difficult.

☐ Eat a healthy, vitamin-rich diet.

☐ Get enough exercise.

☐ When hysterectomy is needed, ask for counselling beforehand.

THE MALE MENOPAUSE

The Things People Say

*'There is no change in men equivalent to the
female climacteric.'*
Dr Brice Pitt, Making the Most of Middle Age

*'If a man knows who he is and is secure in his sense of identity he can
effect his changes successfully and gradually re-establish himself.'*
London psychiatrist

*'The worst part of the male menopause is the realization that your
ambitions are hopeless. Your life is no longer on the fast lane of the
highway. You are no longer twenty-five. Pulling over to the slow lane
makes you feel a failure.'*
Forty-two-year-old New Yorker

*'In at least ninety-eight per cent of men the decline in male hormones
from the age of forty onwards is very gradual and potency and virility
can be maintained for the rest of their lives.'*
Dr Brice Pitt, Making the Most of Middle Age

*'During the midlife crisis a man's sexual capacity is his
greatest concern.'*
James Conway, Men in Midlife Crisis

*'Quality control matters in life and in midlife it's spiritual quality
control that is important.'*
London psychiatrist

*'Survival lies in the ability to spot what is going wrong and make
the correct decisions recognizing the changes you need. . . so that the
future works to your advantage.'*
Geoffrey Aquilina Ross, How to Survive the Male Menopause

*'For success, all future expectations must be reasonable. Men who
take stock of what they have and see they can inject new activities*

into their home life. . . invariably do better than the man. . .
expecting that only by doing something dramatic will he come up
trumps.' Therapist

'It was a time when the main bases of my life — my faith, our
marriage, my sense of purpose — all seemed to shake at once and
called me to think again about who I was, what I was doing, and
where I was going.'
Bishop Jim Thompson, *Half Way*

'Take the male menopause seriously. Make the adjustments you need
and make the most of your life. Do not jeopardize your future.'
Therapist

The male menopause is talked about, joked about and even written about almost as much as the female one. But is there really any such thing?

Since menopause means the end of monthly periods, it certainly cannot be literally applied to men. But is there some kind of comparable change going on in a man's physical and physiological system at about the same age?

The answer, again, is no. In the case of a woman, all the eggs that will be released from her body, at the rate of one a month, are already present when she is born. When no more eggs are ripened and released, she ceases to be fertile. A man, on the other hand, goes on manufacturing sperm continuously during his adult life. Although there is some gradual decline in male hormone production from the age of forty onwards, this does not affect his fertility greatly and a man may father a child well on into old age.

Popular myth connects sexual fertility with sexual potency but in fact there is no such link. In midlife some men complain to their doctor about a loss in sexual ability, afraid that their sexual powers are waning because of their age. But hormone deficiency is only to blame for loss of sexual potency in about one in fifty cases. The real causes are almost always emotional and psychological.

Some doctors do make a practice of prescribing the male hormone, testosterone, to improve sexual performance at this age but, except in the few cases where the testes are not functioning properly, the treatment is worse than useless. It may well be counter-productive, since the introduction of artificial hormones can discourage the body from producing its own natural supply.

Midlife crisis

It is still very clear that in spite of the fact that there is no physiological change at midlife, many men of forty and upwards do experience something very like the feelings that accompany the menopause in women. They may go to the doctor complaining not only about impotence but of hot flushes, fatigue, apathy, nervousness, irritability, palpitations and depression — all symptoms which sound suspiciously like those connected with the menopause. But, as Dr Brice Pitt explains in *Making the Most of Middle Age*, these are 'common manifestations of emotional disturbance — anxiety and depressive states, largely arising from disturbance in relationships, not disturbance in hormones'. All of them can occur at any other time of life, given the same pressures. In other words, the so-called male menopause is the result of extra pressures that arise at this age as well as the inward tension of coming to terms with loss of youth and all that this entails.

Unfortunately for them, men do not always feel able to talk about the negative feelings that they may experience in midlife. Until recently it has not been the custom in our society for men to talk about their deepest emotions. This is especially true when these feelings include admissions of failure, weakness or despair.

Most men were indoctrinated with the belief that brave boys don't cry, from the time that they were toddlers. The hidden message is that, in order to succeed, a man must be in control of his emotions, and if he feels love, pity or sadness strongly he must not let it be seen. Only the more dominant emotions, such as anger, can be safely displayed. At school, any sign of tears would have left a boy open to cries of 'Sissy!' and probably made him the butt of ridicule and bullying.

Not surprisingly, having learned the lesson well, many men are not able to share their feelings of anxiety, despair or inadequacy, even with the person closest to them. Some mothers do help their sons to show emotion within the loving context of family and these lucky ones may find it easier to be honest and open with their wives. But a wife who makes a habit of belittling her husband and criticizing or nagging him is not likely to be at the receiving end of his confidences, especially any admissions of failure or inadequacy. Men are not likely either to confide in a best friend. It does not often seem to be part of male friendship to share on a personal and self-analytical level.

It would be a mistake to imagine that all men are longing to pour out their hearts and unburden their souls to someone else. Many have not reached a point of analyzing their feelings sufficiently to put them into words. Others are not willing to admit to personal failure or loss. They are not only unwilling to talk about negative feelings but unable to admit to them, believing that they have failed as men if they own up to being unsuccessful or inadequate, even to themselves. They may not even be aware of what is troubling them. They are conscious of a general lack of well-being and sense of dis-ease but do not look within themselves for the answer. They are more likely to pin the blame onto some external event or person than on the arrival of midlife and their reactions to it.

Some of the blame can, of course, be laid at the door of outside events or people, and these situations will be discussed fully in the chapters that follow. There are many stress factors in the area of work (see chapters 15 and 16) Home life can also bring pressures at this stage of life. A man may feel trapped by too heavy financial commitments, as well as by his responsibilities for both the younger and older generations. Teenage children can bring their anxieties (see chapters 9–11). A wife going through her own menopausal difficulties may find it hard to understand what her husband is experiencing. If his way of handling his personal problems is to be short-tempered, fault-finding or moody and unresponsive, she may well be unsympathetic.

It is not only outside pressures that cause a man to suffer a midlife crisis. Much of what he experiences is likely to be the result of inward turmoil and questioning. Men, no less than women, are often painfully aware of the ageing process. A man may still *feel* thirty, but a glance in the mirror reveals that his hair is receding, his waistline spreading and his face showing lines of wear. With a jolt he realizes that he has already used up half his allotted life-span. For a man, the crunch may come when he discovers that he can no longer achieve in terms of physical prowess. His teenage children, or nephews and nieces, can beat him at the games he always used to win.

As he looks back over the past twenty years, he may regret some of his choices or grieve for the ambitions he is no longer likely to achieve. A highly successful man, who has made his million or reached the top of his profession, may also feel despair. Many people at midlife need to search for new meaning, for a sense of personal identity and goals that will serve them for the rest of life.

Some men become aware at midlife that they have failed to provide sufficient outlets for their softer emotions over the past twenty or more years. There is not much scope for pity or gentleness in the ruthless world of work. Many couples fail to nurture their marriage, and much of the warmth and tenderness of love has disappeared over the years, along with the romance. If the sexual relationship is successful it may be so only in terms of orgasm rather than in tender mutual commitment. Many men have been too busy to give their children the loving relationship that they need from a father as well as a mother.

The irony of the situation is that the time at which a father realizes his need for a closer and more affectionate relationship with his children may coincide with the time when they are growing away from parental care and leaving home in search of their own independence. Of course there are many men who have always maintained a gentle and loving attitude both at work and at home but there are others who come to value that side of their nature only as they reach midlife.

Changing patterns

At the same time that a man is recognizing the importance of allowing the gentler side of his nature to blossom, his wife is likely to be more aware of the world outside the home and ready to assert her own independence. Women are said to become more aggressive and outward-looking in midlife, particularly if their twenties and thirties have been spent within the home, bringing up the family. It can be hard for a man to come to terms with his wife's new-found self-confidence and financial independence when his own morale has reached a low. She may appear to need him less just when his confidence requires a boost.

Home patterns may change too. If both husband and wife are now out at work all day, there will need to be some rearrangement of duties and routine. It is important for men and women to try to understand the very different reactions to midlife that both are experiencing in this particular area, and for married couples to sit down and work out a new pattern of living that will not merely patch up the problems but actually inject new life and growth into their individual and shared lives (see chapter 13).

The way men react to all these different pressures from without and within will vary enormously. Some, aware of their lost youth, try desperately to put the clock back. There are plenty of jokes about middle-aged men who wear tight jeans, unbuttoned shirts, and hair styles more suited to a twenty-year-old. Sadly, their efforts to look young deceive no one.

Another common reaction to midlife is to seek reassurance by having an affair with a girl — or girls — young enough to be their daughter. The need is often less for sexual satisfaction than for the reassurance that they are still sexually attractive to pretty women. A man whose libido has been diminished by stress or overwork or lack of confidence may have an affair in order to improve his sexual performance. This may have the desired effect. If a man is suffering from low self-esteem and is frequently belittled by his wife, his sexual performance within the marriage may be lowered. Once he begins to be afraid that he won't be able to perform he is increasingly likely to fail. If he is unable to have an erection on one occasion and worries about it, he probably won't be able to next time. An admiring young woman on the other hand, who knows nothing of his self-doubt but sees him as a successful man of the world — perhaps her own boss — may boost his general morale, with the result that he succeeds sexually too.

But, because the root of the trouble is not physical but goes much deeper, an affair is not the real answer to his problems. The price he pays for this temporary solution is a very high one in practical terms, quite apart from any moral consideration. Not only is he threatening his marriage but he is paving the way for a crop of troubles, both at home and with his new partner. She may view the affair very differently from him and is not likely to be satisfied for long to be no more than a means of bolstering a middle-aged man's ego.

Most of us are on our worst behaviour at home with our family, and men with a midlife crisis are no exception. Geoffrey Aquilina Ross, in *How to Survive the Male Menopause* suggests that men at this stage tend to feel trapped by home. They may vary from being listless and dull to being the life and soul of the party when others are around. A normally decisive man may adopt a 'You choose' or 'It doesn't matter' attitude. He may be restless, unable to settle to any one occupation or to finish the jobs in the home that he has begun. (Some wives might think that this tendency is not limited to midlife!)

Health

Health is also a preoccupation for some men in their forties and fifties. Their fears of a coronary or high blood pressure may well be justified by their lifestyle, but it is easier to focus on bodily problems than on the underlying issues, and health worry can be a substitute for taking a hard and honest look at the matters that need dealing with at the deeper levels of personality and relationships. Even so, it is a good idea to have a health check around the age of forty, and some firms arrange such a service for their employees. A healthy diet, sensible exercise and cutting down on food, alcohol and smoking will help a man to look and feel both fitter and younger.

Many men, as well as women, turn to alcohol as a release from the problems of midlife. It is not usually done as a deliberate policy; having a drink helps to ease and deaden immediate worries, at least in the short term. Soon another drink, or a stronger one, becomes necessary to keep worries at bay. The only way to recognize when alcohol is more than a social matter and is fast becoming a dangerous habit, is to compare your own alcohol intake with the recommended safe limits. Alcohol in excess is extremely harmful to body and mind, interfering with work, relationships and family life. It is also useless as a problem solver (see also chapter 4).

One effect of the pressures at this age may be depression (see chapter 5). There is still a reluctance to admit to depression in the sense of a recognized illness, rather than feeling blue. Many people who have had no intimate contact with the illness are still insensitive, and assume that depressed people need only to pull their socks up and learn to cope like everyone else. It can be harder for a man to admit to the apparent, though not real, 'failure' of suffering from depression than for a woman. The good news is that those coming through depression have almost always, in the process, recognized the underlying causes of overwork, anger, guilt or loss that triggered the illness, and have come to terms with them in a way that many others fail to do. They have probably reached far greater maturity than those who criticize or patronize them for being inadequate.

Positive ways forward

In spite of the negative aspects of the male menopause, the effects can be wholly good and beneficial. There are positive ways through in all the areas discussed and the changes to be made can work to everyone's advantage. For a married man there is the opportunity where necessary to rescue the marriage from a state of boredom and arrested development, where it may have stuck fast years before. If husband and wife have the will to do so, they may bring the marriage up to date, so that it fits their present needs and is a living and satisfying relationship.

In the area of work, it may be difficult or impossible to negotiate change, but at least most men can try to achieve a more balanced life, with some room for physical and mental recreation. Hobbies and interests developed at this age will bring further scope in the more leisured years ahead. Allowing the caring and compassionate side of their nature an outlet through the work of some local group or church care scheme, brings as many rewards to the carers as to those at the receiving end.

There is also a need to nurture the spiritual dimension of life, which may have been neglected during adult life or never even explored. Midlife often makes people more keenly aware of the pointlessness of a life based only on material and selfish achievements. Bishop Jim Thompson, writing from his own experience, says in his book *Half Way*:

'There are indeed several disciplines which illuminate our understanding of midlife, such as psychology, sociology and medicine, but I believe that faith, too, has much to offer. Without the dimension of God, the analysis and the answers are stunted. . . Of course, religion can be a most neurotic response to life, but it is not necessarily so. All those who deny its possibility will have to accept responsibility — if God turns out to be true — that they cut off many a needy human being from the resources of faith, its knowledge, its healing, its strength, its forgiveness, which none of their technology and medicine were able to replace. . . Religious insights are essential to the passage through midlife, facing, as they do, questions of identity and meaning. I make no apology for thinking that theology has a significant part to play.'

And neither do I.

ACTION CHECKPOINTS

☐ Try to acknowledge feelings of loss or inadequacy.

☐ Try to discuss problems with one other person.

☐ Work on marriage relationship.

☐ Eat less.

☐ Drink less.

☐ Take more exercise.

☐ Arrange routine medical check-up.

☐ Explore the spiritual dimension of life.

SECTION 2
HEALTH AND BEAUTY

3
BEAUTY WITHIN

The Things People Say

'Life isn't equal. Life isn't fair. Some women are short, some women are tall, some women are fat, some are thin. They're all different. It depends what you do with it.'
Anoushka Hempel, hotel owner and couturier

'My husband admires older women and always enjoys talking to them at parties. He says that even their faces are more interesting.'
Thirty-five-year-old woman

'This beautiful woman has energy, a sense of self, humour, a generosity of spirit, kindness and is dedicated to making herself the best person she can be. That is a beautiful woman.'
Victoria Principal, *The Beauty Principal*

'We will be happier if we accept the natural characteristics and limitations of the stages through which our bodies pass. There is a beauty to every stage of life.'
Jim Thompson, Bishop of Stepney, *Half Way*

'Stop for a minute before your mirror, five minutes before your soul, and fifteen before your God.'
Michel Quoist

'It took me years to understand that beauty is not looking like someone else. . . being beautiful is feeling happy inside and being honest about myself.'
Victoria Principal, *The Beauty Principal*

'If you learn to use your mind as well as you can use a powder-puff you will become more truly beautiful.'
Sophia Loren, *Women and Beauty*

Beauty is said to be in the eye of the beholder and many of us who are over forty, beholding our own image in the mirror, don't much like what we see. We either walk away quickly or peer more closely, resolving to start at once on a campaign to get rid of wrinkles, eliminate grey hairs and introduce a new nightly beauty routine.

Some of us may never have been very happy with our bodies. Perhaps we were not born with genes that gave us the vital statistics and facial characteristics currently fashionable. But most young people who wish to do so learn to adapt their looks in order to conform as far as possible to the popular image — witness the number of Princess Diana look-alikes. As well as looking good, in contemporary terms, young people have a freshness and vitality which is lovely in itself.

But something more is needed to make a person beautiful, over and above the attractiveness of youth, basic good looks and skilful make-up. Attractiveness, even in someone young, depends on more than nature plus art. A girl may have the best features possible yet pass unnoticed in a crowd unless she has a personality which brings her beauty to life.

It seems to me that something that comes from within a person, something more important than outward beauty, is needed in order to turn heads and call forth comments — but that may be a middle-aged judgment, because as we get older we want increasingly to see some sign that beauty is more than skin-deep. We wish to glimpse the soul inside the body beautiful.

It is certainly true that the older we grow, the more other people will be aware of the person behind our outward image. Our personality and the character we have acquired will be apparent, rather than mere physical looks, making us glowing and attractive, or cold and unprepossessing. The impression that others form will not depend on expensive clothes, clever make-up, or even on natural good features. It is said — rather alarmingly — that after you are forty your face is of your own making. The kind of person you have grown to be has left its clear imprint on the set of the mouth, the expression of the eyes, and the lines of the face.

Try studying the faces of any middle-aged men or women travelling with you in the train, or standing near you at the supermarket check-out. It is possible to read something of the way they react to life, and even to guess at their life history, from tell-tale signs of face and body. Of course, it is also possible to make mistakes. Pain, rather than a sour nature, may be the cause of tightly drawn lips and hard-set jaw. We cannot always be held responsible for the way we look.

The good news at midlife is that the tell-tale wrinkles and grey hairs that make depressing viewing in the mirror do not tell the whole story, or even the most important part. By the time we reach midlife, we can stop the struggle to capture a particular style of good looks and relax in the knowledge that the person we are is far more important than accidents of birth or artful make-up and cosmetic surgery.

It is possible to go on spending time and money on externals, but to achieve a beauty that will last into middle age and old age too, we need to begin to spend time on the beauty that begins at the deepest level of our character and personality and leaves its imprint on our faces.

It is also important to learn how to make the most of our looks and our bodies at this new stage of life, and there are plenty of books and magazine articles giving helpful advice. The remaining chapters in this section will also deal with that subject. But I have searched in vain for comments on the art of inward beauty in those same books and articles. Perhaps the subject is avoided because inward beauty is even more costly to achieve than the most expensive course of treatment at a beauty clinic. Honest self-appraisal and an openness to change is a high price to pay.

We may avoid the subject of inner beauty because we belong to a society that pays very little attention to the importance of character–building and spiritual values. The qualities of compassion, loyalty, self-sacrifice and patience, for example, sound distinctly old-fashioned. We also live in an age that demands instant results and solutions. Character-forming takes time and it is not usually possible to change the effects of resentment, discontent and hardness overnight, when they represent half a lifetime of habitual reaction. Lines of laughter and loving, as well as lines of hate and fear, are etched gradually on our faces. Our customary attitudes are betrayed by our whole bearing as well as our faces, and more than our pocket will need to be touched if we want them to change.

But even an old person's face can be changed when he or she is transformed from within. We may have witnessed the profound difference that the experience of loving or being loved can bring about in a person's looks, as well as in the whole way that they carry themselves. God's love, received and experienced by a man or woman, can transform them within and without even more dramatically and permanently than any human love can do. Many people demonstrate in their whole bearing as well as in their looks, the fact that they have experienced God's love, his forgiveness of the past and the peace of heart he gives in the present and for the future.

Eliminate the negative

There are a good many 'don'ts' when we set about following a health and beauty regime. There are some definite don'ts, in the same way, in the area of inward health and beauty. Our minds, as well as our bodies, need a healthy diet and enough exercise. We probably don't feed on constant violence or pornography, but we may have picked up the habit of grumbling, criticizing — or even of being absorbed with very petty and small affairs.

Of course, much of life is concerned with trivia, but unless we are careful we can become literally small-minded, by constantly dwelling on matters of little or no importance. In the end, it really isn't a matter of life and death that someone has parked their car in our way, or that the dog next door has broken one of the shrubs. When small matters fill our minds, and we become obsessed with the trivial and unimportant, our minds and affections wither and shrink.

There are plenty of good books in the local library that will help enlarge our outlook and add breadth to our interests. There are radio programmes that stimulate the imagination. It is better to listen to programmes like these while we do routine jobs than to brood on small concerns. A mind that is fresh and lively transforms the body too. Similarly, although it is natural that the affairs of our own family circle should figure largely in our thinking and planning, when such concerns are all that fill the mind, our world has become too small and we are the poorer.

Some habits of thinking are wholly negative and damaging to spirit, mind and body. Worry, anger, guilt and fear are some examples of these negative emotions.

Dr Leslie Weatherhead, writing over thirty years ago in his book *Prescription for Anxiety*, puts forward some positive ways to combat negative thoughts. He suggests that when we really grasp the fact that God loves us — unconditionally — it sets us free from the prison of fear and self-doubt. God's love is not dependent on our niceness, or our deserving, nor on our successes or our failures. He loves us just as we are and is willing to get to work on us at the deepest level of our subconscious, as well as our conscious, minds. He can deal — if we will let him — with the guilt and worry that trap us and can help us to find a way through the problems and circumstances that overwhelm us.

W. D. Kendall, who is quoted by Dr Weatherhead, uses the analogy of a pocket torch compared to an electric light fitting: 'The torch is self-contained, having a battery of its own which sooner or later becomes exhausted and the torch useless. The electric light, on the other hand, is wired up to a power station from which it receives an unfailing source of supply. . . We habitually think of ourselves as being like the torch with a self-contained and definitely limited supply of vitality, intelligence and reserve of power. . . which may become exhausted.' Instead, when we are in touch with God, we are connected to an inexhaustible supply. Our circumstances and problems may not change but our capacity to cope with them will.

Accentuate the positive

When we fill our minds with plenty to interest and stimulate them, and foster a positive attitude to ourselves, to others and to the circumstances of life, the good effects will extend to our bodies too. Without realizing it, we shall *look* more alive and more attractive.

One good habit, particularly necessary as we reach midlife, is to learn to accept changes in age and circumstance. Acceptance is not a popular concept today because it is often interpreted as bowing weakly to life when a little more effort and determination would alter the case. In a situation where taking action will improve circumstances for everyone concerned, acceptance of the status quo is obviously wrong. But there are times when no amount of protest and action will bring about the desired change. Growing older is a case in point. Many people have pushed back the boundaries of youth and, as one young man commented, 'The forty-year-old today looks a lot better than the forty-year-old of twenty years ago.' But midlife and old age are still inevitable.

Accepting that fact for ourselves may be difficult. When we are young we have the illusion that everyone in our small circle has always been the particular age at which we know them. Our parents seem always to have been middle-aged and our grandparents always old. Their stories of childhood have a fascination for us, by their sheer improbability. They are the old, but we are the young.

Since each of us continues to feel the same person inside, we find it hard to accept the fact that life is changing, not static, and that we are no longer the young ones but have arrived at a new stage and age-group. Most people are also unwilling to accept the consequences of such mental recognition.

Perhaps acceptance is particularly difficult for those who are today in their forties. Steve Turner, in a series of articles in *The Times* about those born in the immediate post-war years, wrote: 'The baby-boomer can never quite forget the horrifying prospect that middle age was made out to be during the years of his or her youth.' He also quotes Dr Dan Kiley, a US psychologist, who suggested that men and women who grew up in the sixties sometimes suffer from the Peter Pan syndrome: 'The idea developed in the sixties,' he suggests, 'that youth was not something to pass through on the way to adulthood but something to stay in.'

If we are to live the second half of our lives in a fulfilled and appropriate way, we need to make the correct adjustment and accept the fact that our youth has gone. But accepting is not another word for being merely resigned to the inevitable. It may involve resigning ourselves to the loss of what has passed, but acceptance has a much more positive connotation. The main emphasis is on accepting, not the losses, but all that the new phase in life has to offer. Once midlife is accepted in this sense, it begins to be a time of fulfilment and of new opportunities and enjoyments.

Flexibility is another positive inward attitude that will affect the way we look. Middle-aged people are sometimes accused of being rigid and unable to adapt. A mind that is open to new ideas and willing to admit to mistakes, to go on learning and to discover better ways of doing things will not have the set features and hard expression of the person who has made up their mind once for all. Readiness to change our opinions about other people is also important. Keeping a mind open to see their good points and to revise adverse judgments, as well as to give them the benefit of the doubt, softens our features as well as our attitude of mind. Readiness to learn and to change will keep us young in heart as well as younger looking.

Something new

'I really feel that I should be taking up a few hobbies, like bird-watching,' a contented forty-year-old remarked the other day. And she had the right idea.

Although most men and women are still working to full capacity at this stage, midlife is a good time to increase mental and emotional horizons as much as possible, so that there will be no premature withering and shrivelling of capacities. If we have always had a smouldering interest in archaeology or music, painting or photography, now is the time to begin to explore and foster it — even if free time is limited.

Fortunately, the success of many people at seventy and beyond in academic and creative achievement has exploded the myth that we can ever be too old to learn or to express ourselves creatively. It is not a pipe-dream to consider taking a degree or beginning to paint in oils when retirement comes, and a foray into the chosen subject at this stage, to whet the appetite, relieves the heavy strains of the midlife years and gives aim and purpose for the freer years that still lie in the future.

Some people in midlife miss the opportunity for giving care to others, either because it has not been their lot to bring up a family or look after elderly parents, or because, those responsibilities past, they now have skills and emotional energy to spare. There are many openings for such carers, either on a weekly or occasional basis, in connection with local groups or churches (see chapter 16).

Those unable to spare regular time might be able to give a week's leave in order, for example, to accompany a group of physically or mentally disabled people on holiday. One middle-aged widow who has done this a number of times, told me that it was the happiest week of her year, full of fun and laughter. The severely physically disabled people that she was with had learned how to take from others, and to find humour even in their own limitations. They had, in fact, achieved a maturity that many who are able-bodied have still not found. This volunteer discovered, as so many do, that she set out to give but received far more in return.

Look on the bright side

The response of thankfulness, which many less fortunate people seem to have learned, is one of the most important ways of reacting at this stage of life, as it is at any other. It is particularly easy to get into the habit of grumbling and complaining at midlife. When we are feeling generally under the weather, or suffering mood changes which are hard to understand, as well as coping with burdens and pressures of many different kinds, we find it only too easy to look on the black side and feel hard done by. But almost every situation contains seeds of good as well as bad and choosing to highlight the positive or the negative aspects of our lot in life can soon become a habit. At the risk of sounding corny, I have to confess the difference it has made to me when, instead of lying awake counting my worries, I have followed the old-fashioned advice of counting blessings. The Bible instructs us to be thankful, and as a Christian I am glad of that. I am sure that one reason for this rule is the beneficial effect of being thankful to the person concerned. There is nothing quite like it for restoring a sense of proportion, lifting the heart above the minor ills and miseries and thereby smoothing the furrowed brow! However bad things are, it is amazing how many pluses life still offers and, when God is also at work in the situation, it is my experience that there is always something to say thank you for.

Before he became a Christian, Malcolm Muggeridge went to Calcutta to film a programme for the BBC about Mother Teresa. When the cameraman saw how poor the light was inside her home for the dying, he doubted whether anything at all would come out on the film. But to the amazement of everyone, including the cameraman, 'this particular footage came out very well,' Muggeridge recorded in *Something Beautiful for God*, 'showing the home for the dying. . . bathed in a soft and very beautiful light. There has been some dispute over this. My own feeling was, and remains, that love carried to the point that Mother Teresa has carried it, has its own luminosity, and that the medieval painters, who showed saints with halos, were not so far wide of the mark as a twentieth-century mind might suppose.'

Few of us could hope to generate the peace and love of God in such a palpable way, but we can learn from Mother Teresa and from others less well-known who also radiate the beauty that comes from within. Many sociologists and psychologists teach a two-dimensional understanding of men and women, involving body and mind. But such an interpretation is too limited to cover the facts.

Unless the spiritual dimension is reckoned with, there is no way of finding the kind of satisfaction that meets our deepest needs. Most of us ignore our spiritual nature and give ourselves no time in which to seek and commune with God. Mother Teresa points us to the importance of inner quiet: 'We need to find God and he cannot be found in noise and restlessness. God is the friend of silence . . . the more we receive in silent prayer, the more we can give in our active life.'

But silence and the time to be quiet are expensive commodities in our society and in the patterns of most lives. Another writer gives a goal that the busiest of us could find attainable, if we have a mind to do so: 'Build into your day little enclosures of silence; they spill over into your life and bring peace, the peace of God.'

ACTION CHECKPOINTS

☐ Keep a well-stocked mind.

☐ Enlarge interests.

☐ List things to be thankful for.

☐ Reserve times to be quiet.

☐ Provide for spiritual, as well as physical and mental, hunger.

4
KEEPING A HEALTHY BODY

The Things People Say

'Middle life is a time for making all sorts of adjustments and adaptations. It is also a time for reviewing your attitude to your health and well-being.'
Dr Jean Coope, *The Menopause*

'There's plenty of evidence to show that getting a little puffed and increasing your heart rate is good for you. Doctors agree that there are no risks in regular exercise, as long as you start gently and gradually build up to the more strenuous activities.'
The Sports Council

'Eating for the benefit of your health doesn't mean chewing your way through mounds of bran and raw carrots. Healthy food can and should be delicious.'
Living Today leaflet

'Obesity is one of the most common, important and avoidable causes of ill-health in the middle-aged and older in the civilized world.' A doctor

'Glandular changes can make some people gain weight at the menopause but the commonest cause is eating and drinking more than you need.'
Dr Jean Coope, *The Menopause*

'I've always had a battle with my weight. When I had the children I put on lots of weight which I never really lost. It's not the quantity I eat — sweet things are my downfall.'
Working wife and mother

'The big question is: do you really want to stop smoking? Because this is the key to success. Make up your mind you are going to stop, and you will.'
Health Education Council booklet

'Once you think you've got it licked, you're in trouble. Alcoholism is a chronic, progressive and sometimes fatal disease.'
Former US First Lady, Betty Ford

The modern trend in medicine — like the ancient biblical view — is to see human beings as whole people, recognizing that it is bad practice to treat separate parts of a person without looking at the total man or woman. The mind and emotions are involved as well as the body and any physical symptoms of illness that may be present.

In practice, many doctors are too busy to take a long hard look at every patient. Too often it's still a matter of exit patient, clutching a prescription for aches, pains and infections. In this book, spiritual, mental and emotional well-being come first in this section on health and beauty, because caring for the needs of the inner person is not only of primary importance in itself but is also a great step towards achieving physical well-being. Of course we also have to recognize that in the kind of world in which we live, it is possible to have inward peace and security and yet to suffer from various problems with our bodies. In fact the process may work in reverse. Physical pain may affect our tranquillity and peace of mind, so that the mind reacts to the body as well as the body to the mind. Our job is to keep every part of us as healthy as possible, for the good of the whole person.

When we reach midlife, our bodies need a bit more care than when we were younger. Someone, rather unkindly, has used the analogy of a car that needs more servicing when it is no longer fresh from the showroom. Well-person clinics, where men and women around the forty mark can have tests to check their physical fitness, already exist. But until preventive medicine becomes cheaper and more readily available, most of us must rely on our own common sense and on the reliable information which is available in order to keep ourselves running smoothly.

When we feel good we look good, so much that is said about health might equally well come under the heading of beauty. Health of body, health of mind and beauty are divided into separate chapters here only for the sake of giving information in a readily accessible way. In order to feel well and look our best and most beautiful, all the chapters in this section need to be considered as part of a whole.

Eating to keep fit

'You are what you eat' is a favourite maxim, and eating the right things is important in order to be healthy at every stage of life. The problem is, what is good to eat and what is harmful? Fashions change at an alarming rate and at any given time experts hold differing views. One honest booklet on food and health explains, 'The main reason why there are conflicting views about the effect of food on health is that we simply don't know all the answers yet. Research over the past years has begun to answer lots of questions, but much still remains to be sorted out. And until that time, it is inevitable that experts and commentators will interpret the interim results in different ways.'* At the end of 1986 a group of professors, doctors and nutritionists in Britain produced a book repudiating 'crude and simplistic propaganda' about foods alleged to be healthy and unhealthy. Those concerned were anxious that instead of recommending or condemning whole ranges of foods outright, balanced, moderate eating patterns should be encouraged.

The message seems to be that the best diet is one where as many different foods as possible are included and where meals are planned to include:

• bread — at least half should be wholemeal

• pulses, such as peas and kidney beans

• rice and pasta, especially brown or wholemeal

• oatmeal or high fibre breakfast cereal

• skimmed or semi-skimmed milk

• fish — both white and oily

• very lean meat

• poultry — but without the skin

• eggs

• lots of different vegetables (including potatoes) and fruit

Another way of putting across the same kind of message is:

• eat plenty of fresh fruit and vegetables.

*Living Today, No 1, published by Sainsbury.

- eat plenty of fibre-rich foods.

- cut down on fat, sugar and salt.

- get plenty of variety in what you eat.

This kind of eating is easy, whether cooking for a family, for two or for one. Leaving potatoes unpeeled and providing fresh fruit instead of fat- and sugar-rich puddings is a great time-saver. It's good to know that the easiest snack in the world — baked beans on (wholemeal) toast is also doing you good and not costing much in money or preparation time. Most doctors and nutritionists would agree that cutting down on fat, especially animal fat, and sugar are two good rules for eating in midlife, even though not all agree that positive proof of their harmful effects is conclusive.

Eating to lose weight

When we are fat, losing weight is important for our health but it is also a great boost to morale to feel more attractive because we have managed to shed surplus pounds. In this chapter the emphasis is on the importance to health of keeping within certain weight limits.

Guides to ideal weight often seem arbitrary and inflexible. It helps to know whether you have a small, medium or large frame. For women, the average circumference of the wrist is eight inches/20cm and of the ankle nine-and-a-half inches/24cm. The pelvis, measured across the front of the stomach between the two bony hip points you can feel with your fingers, is on average nine inches. If you are below or above these measurements, your build tends towards one end or other of the average frame size.

It isn't fair!

People who don't put on weight take it for granted that the rest of us are greedy and lacking in will power. While it is a fact that we often eat much more than we imagine we do (try writing down everything you eat over a period of a week and prove the point), it is a fact that some people put on weight far more quickly than others. Research has shown what most of us have always known, that people can be divided into two groups, 'easy weight gainers' and 'hard weight gainers'. When it comes to achieving the right weight for health, and maintaining it, some of us are going to have a far harder task than others.

Being overweight is dangerous. Overall it lowers life expectancy and among other things increases the risk of high blood pressure, diabetes, heart disease, gallstones and gout. And, as if that is not enough, it causes extra problems for joints of knees, hips and lower back, causing osteoarthritis and aggravating the condition where it already exists. Breathing is affected and bronchitis is more likely to occur in overweight people.

By midlife our bodies become less efficient at burning up calories. Women — rather unfairly I feel — tend to burn up calories less efficiently than men. A little bit of excess weight — say five or ten pounds — is not considered harmful, but for those who are seriously overweight or who need to lose some pounds because of their medical condition, the problem is knowing what diet to follow. Doctors generally agree in warning us against:

- crash diets

- cranky diets

- low-carbohydrate diets

- low-calorie diets

- high-fat diets

- low-fluid diets

In many cases, the long-term effect of such diets is to replace all the pounds lost and some of the diets may be positively dangerous. Far better to change eating habits so that a sensible pattern is established, easing up when a satisfactory weight is reached, but still keeping to the same 'right' kind of foods. It is better to lose a steady two or three pounds a week than to achieve a drastic weight loss more dramatically, only to replace the lost pounds a few months later.

There are any number of sensible diets set out in paperbacks or reputable magazine supplements, many of them suggesting specimen meals for a week or a month. Some menus are expensive or not realistic for those also cooking for a hungry family, so it is a matter of choosing a programme that suits your lifestyle and purse. All aim to restrict calorie intake but most allow for one small treat a day, such as a small glass of dry wine or a chocolate biscuit.

Here are some medically recommended guidelines from which you can plan your own menus:

Every day eat at least:

- one helping of one of the following: lean meat, white fish, poultry, cheese, nuts

- one helping of: brown cereals, wholemeal bread, potatoes

- two helpings of one of the following: green vegetables, a large mixed salad, fruit

- one pint of fluid such as: water, soup, low calorie drink, lemon tea

Remember that how you cook food is also important. Cut out frying or use minimal fat in a non-stick pan. Steam or microwave vegetables to retain vitamins and flavour. Women may have problems keeping weight down at the time of the menopause and after, and men and businesswomen have their own difficulties if their work involves a good deal of sitting at a desk or car wheel, and giving or receiving hospitality lunches. They will need to find ways of shedding the accumulated pounds.

Exercise

Some pessimists have calculated that enormous exercise workouts would be needed in order to achieve even modest weight loss, but it is now recognized that exercise does effectively help to burn up calories by speeding up the body's metabolic rate for some time afterwards. This is especially true of vigorous games of squash or fast running. In general, the gentler the exercise, the less it is an aid to slimming.

But exercise is an important part of keeping fit for many other reasons. It lessens the risk of coronary heart disease, is good for lungs as well as heart, keeps muscles and bones healthy and in women helps to prevent osteoporosis (thinning of the bones). It also neutralizes the ill effects of sitting at a desk all day and eating large lunches. A bout of exercise of any kind is a wonderful outlet for the frustrations that build up during the day and it helps to release tension and enable us to relax.

The golden rule is to begin gently and not to plunge into a sudden regime of vigorous exercise. Those over forty should build up slowly over several months before arriving at a suggested target of half an hour three times a week of vigorous exercise, which can include dancing, squash, tennis, running, or energetic swimming. Gentle exercise is valuable too but needs to be taken most days in order to do us real good.

Those of us who feel we are too busy or not dedicated enough to set aside time for exercise periods can utilize our daily routine to provide at least some opportunities to keep fit.

Walking or cycling to work or to the station instead of using the car, and exercising the dog regularly (breathing deeply and keeping a good posture as we walk), are ways of incorporating exercise into the normal schedule. Household duties provide plenty of bending and stretching, which can be consciously made the most of. A group of American housewives discussed how they combined an exercise routine with everyday living and one recommended her method of keeping a pan which she constantly used on a high shelf, so that she did plenty of stretching every day. For almost everyone, whatever their age, circumstances or disability, some kind of exercise is appropriate and healthy. Exercise tones you up all over and as well as making you feel fresher and fitter, it helps you to sleep better.

People who work in an office may have their own particular problems. Midlife is a time when the results of bad posture can cause trouble. Check that the desk is the right height and that you can use the equipment on it without straining. 'Sit tall' instead of slouching. Get fresh air and some exercise whenever possible.

Sleep

Most of us need less sleep as we get older — perhaps five or six hours a night instead of eight. It is reassuring to remember that fact when we lie awake worrying about how we are going to feel next day. Sleeping tablets are not recommended, partly because the kind of sleep that they induce is not thought to include the dream sleep that our bodies and minds urgently need. A very occasional half tablet might be prescribed by the doctor to restore a habit of good sleep that has been broken. Normally, for those in good health, it is better to rely on one or more of the commonsense aids to a good night's sleep.

• Unwind before going to bed — TV, radio, crossword, light reading, taking the dog for a walk, listening to music, etc. can all help.

• Don't go to bed hungry — a warm milky drink may help.

• Take a warm, not hot, bath.

• Sort out any matters that are bothering you, or make a list of people to phone or write to, shopping to be done, etc. next day.

• Get enough exercise during the day to be physically as well as mentally tired.

• Make sure that you are the right temperature; that you have enough air; that mattress and pillows are comfortable.

• Put right any relationships that need sorting out; be at peace with God, yourself and others.

• Commit yourself to God's care — reading a Bible verse helps many people.

Lying awake in the small hours, after falling asleep quickly, can become another maddening habit. Worrying about your problems, which seem larger than life at that time of night, is hard to resist. So too is worrying about being awake for so long. Some people who sleep alone read, do a crossword, or listen to the radio for a while. Others get up, without disturbing their sweetly sleeping partner, and do jobs — anything from planting out seedlings to preparing books for the auditors! The least productive thing to do is to keep trying to go to sleep. Accept the wakefulness, finding your own alternative to being asleep, and sleep, in its own contrary way, is more likely to come. And at least you will not have worn yourself out with unavailing efforts.

Some women suffer from sleeplessness during the meno-pause and return to more regular sleep patterns later on. Disturbed sleep patterns may also be one symptom of depres-sion, which requires medical help. When the depression is cured, sleep will return to normal too.

Smoking

An Australian visitor was surprised at the number of people still smoking in Britain and the areas where smoking is allowed. In the large university where he teaches in Australia smoking is banned in all rooms, including common-rooms and refectories. And no one complains. Those who champion smokers' rights should surely recognize that non-smokers, including babies and children, may be harmfully affected by other people being free to smoke in public places. The arguments against smoking range from unpleasant effects — breath, skin, hair and clothes that smell of stale smoke, stained teeth, irritable cough — to health danger: lung cancer, heart disease and chronic bron-chitis. The financial as well as the health cost is high.

In order to give up smoking successfully a person must genuinely want to do so. Parents may be motivated by the fact that a child whose father or mother smokes is far more likely to smoke too. They may also feel that they have no right to put their children at risk by making them passive smokers. They will also consider the risks of a habit that could lead to their own early illness or death.

There are various clinics and self-help groups to support and encourage those wanting to kick the habit; but a lot of determination will be needed to get through the first difficult weeks or months. Advisers say:

• Don't try to give up at a time when you are already stressed.

• Be realistic about how difficult it is going to be.

• Stop altogether — don't try cutting down gradually.

• Resist friends' invitations to 'try just one' — even six months later.

• Don't despair if you've tried before and failed. It often takes more than one attempt. Try again! A sympathetic doctor may help and so will friends and family ready to give support and put up with unreasonable behaviour for the first few weeks or more.

Alcohol dependence

Medical opinion is still divided on whether alcoholism is a disease, possibly inherited, or whether an alcoholic only lacks will-power in order to stop drinking. The World Health Organization has recognized alcoholism as a disease since 1951, and the American Medical Association for nearly as long, but in a recent court case the US Government argued that alcoholism results from excessive drinking 'chosen freely'. It states that 'even those medical authorities who label alcoholism a "disease" concede that it is a disease that can and does involve significant elements of volition'.

A drink problem is less to do with enjoying alcohol than with using it as a means of coping with pressures of various kinds. It is suggested that men become addicted to alcohol as a result of two quite different situations at work. Those who are climbing the career ladder fast may use alcohol as a booster to help them to achieve, and those who recognize that they have failed to reach the top may also turn to alcohol, in an attempt to bolster their failing self-image. Women are becoming more prone to alcohol dependence, either through similar career demands or because of loneliness, boredom or the heavy demands made by family and older relatives. The fact that alcohol can be bought in every supermarket has made it far easier to come by, especially for housewives and young people.

Alcohol can be a source of enjoyment but it is a drug with extremely serious side effects. Excessive drinking can affect:

● liver — death rates due to cirrhosis of the liver are steadily rising

● stomach — inflammation leading to peptic ulcers, and a slowed rate of healing

● heart — can become fatty and heart muscles may be weakened, causing heart failure

The effects of too much alcohol are not limited to the person who drinks. Efficiency at work is decreased and judgment impaired, with possible serious results. The terrible toll of road deaths is heavily weighted by the number of drivers who have been drinking. Drunken pedestrians can cause accidents too.

Drinking affects personal relationships, causing marriage breakdown and harming the children in the family.

Alcoholism is an illness that needs urgent treatment. There are groups such as Alcoholics Anonymous who are able to help, and a limited number of hospitals and clinics where treatment can be given. But it is essential for the man or woman to be prepared to admit that they have a drink problem and be ready to receive help, if there is to be any cure.

What's the limit?

Most people make the change from occasional social drinking to alcohol dependence gradually. Because of the added pressures that often occur at work and in the family at midlife, people are particularly at risk of increasing their drinking at this stage. The only reliable way to calculate how much you are actually having is to keep a diary for a week, noting how much you drink, where you drink it and with whom. A 'standard' drink is calculated as one of the following:

● half a pint of beer

● glass of wine

● small glass of sherry

● single measure of spirits

● quarter pint of strong cider

A suggested sensible limit is:

● for men two or three pints, or their equivalent, two or three times a week

- for women two or three standard drinks, two or three times a week

There are many occasions when no drink at all should be the rule, particularly when driving, operating machinery or taking certain medicines.

It is also important to remember that upper safety limits depend on the person concerned. Women are more affected by alcohol than men. Their lower body water content means that the alcohol is less diluted. A woman's liver is also more readily damaged by alcohol than a man's. Individuals also differ in their alcohol tolerance.

The choice to go without alcohol altogether is a real and valid one. More people are providing non-alcoholic drinks in their homes and at parties for the sake of those driving, and it is possible to invent a whole range of interesting and appetizing non-alcoholic drinks that are absolutely free from lethal side effects.

When to see the doctor

Certain diseases are particularly associated with middle life. When men and women reach forty, they may fear increased possibility of suffering strokes, heart attacks, or high blood pressure. Some doctors advise check-ups at this age but most of us wait to visit the surgery until we suspect something is actually wrong.

If you are anxious about your blood pressure, go to the doctor rather than a department store where the service may be offered. There are also machines on sale for measuring blood pressure, to be used at home. The best medical advice is that only a qualified medical person should make the check. Apart from anything else, readings can be misleading to the uninitiated. Physical exercise or anxiety can cause inaccurate readings. The medical name for high blood pressure is hypertension. It is not a disease in itself, but a condition which may give rise to problems if not controlled.

Anyone with chest pains should also go to the doctor, especially if the pain goes down the arm.

No one can guarantee a way of avoiding heart disease but the risks can be greatly reduced. Doctors advise:

- don't smoke

- eat healthily

- take regular exercise

- go easy on alcohol

- avoid stress when possible

To avoid hypertension the single most important action is probably to lose weight. There is some evidence that salt is bad and many people have cut salt intake in recent years. Smoking is out and so is too much alcohol. In fact, the healthy eating rules that apply to everyone, stand us in good stead for preventing high blood pressure and heart disease.

Osteoarthritis (sometimes called osteoarthrosis by doctors) is another common complaint of midlife, often more troublesome for women at the menopause and afterwards. It is one of many forms of rheumatism and is thought to be the result of wear and tear on joint surfaces, particularly hips, knees and spine. Research indicates that there may be other causes which could explain why younger women also suffer from what should be an elderly person's complaint.

Although there is no known cure for osteoarthritis, there are some ways of making it less of a problem to ordinary living. It is very important to keep weight down so that there is no extra strain on joints. Doctors may prescribe anti-inflammatory drugs to control both inflammation and pain. Gentle exercise, heat, warm baths and pain killers may all help to keep the pain within manageable bounds. Physiotherapy may help, and various forms of alternative medicine, particularly acupuncture, can give pain relief. It is always important to consult a practitioner who has qualifications recognized by your doctor.

Learning to live with pain

Aches and pains sometimes ease up when the menopause is over but many of us will have to settle for a certain amount of back pain, headaches and limited movement from now on. We may not be able to digest foods as easily as we once could. We may find that provided we are not too tired or hard pressed we can manage nicely, but particular weak spots flare up when we overdo things.

Coping with minor ills is very much a matter of learning how to live with them, making small but helpful adjustments to our way of life without letting the complaint loom too large or take over our lifestyle. A rheumatologist told me that his aim was to enable his patients to go on living their particular chosen lifestyle with the least possible hindrance and pain. Normality should be our aim too, but spartan endurance in the face of pain is not the answer.

When back pain and arthritis are the problems it can help to take short rests or breaks from a long stint in one position — say sitting at a desk or standing at an ironing-table. Find the right balance between enough exercise and enough rest. Make sure that your mattress is firm enough and your pillow comfortable. If you have to carry a heavy load, divide the weight between two bags. Learn the right way to get out of bed, and to pick up a heavy object. Find out what gives you pain relief — hot baths and heated pads or cold packs (a bag of peas from the freezer will do nicely). No one is going to want to hear about your aches and pains, but that is no reason why you should suffer more than is necessary. Don't make a fuss but don't be a martyr. Get any medical help available, then set about finding your own way to manage your disabilities. Plenty of other people, unknown to you, are doing exactly the same.

ACTION CHECKPOINTS

If necessary (be honest) —

☐ Eat less.

☐ Drink less alcohol.

☐ Cut out smoking.

☐ Check your diet against healthy food recommendations and adjust where necessary.

☐ Adjust cooking methods for healthier eating.

☐ Get more exercise.

☐ Go for a medical check if necessary.

☐ Check if mattress and pillows need renewing — for better sleep and relief of aches and stiffness.

☐ Come to terms with minor health problems and take time to learn how to manage them.

5
KEEPING A HEALTHY MIND

The Things People Say

'I was forty-five. We had been on holiday in Scotland and I was doing the washing on the Monday when suddenly a huge black cloud seemed to descend — a mass of fear, anxiety and utter depression.'
A housewife

'Smoking tobacco, drinking excess alcohol and taking drugs of dependence. . . should be stopped or severely curtailed. They are false friends because they provide the illusion of temporary relief from stress, while in reality making the processes of defence and successful adaptation much more difficult.'
Coping with Stress

'Stress, in my opinion, is the most significant negative factor at work in modern society.'
Dr Richard Ecker, *The Stress Myth*

'What is stress? Anything that makes you tense, angry, frustrated or miserable.'
Dr G. Wilkinson, *Coping with Stress*

'Midlife is a time when suppressed emotions tend to come to the surface. They have been there over years and many of the established patterns of reaction are demanding to be looked at.'
Doctor and therapist

'Depression is as universal as the common cold. It can be so slight as to be hardly worth the name. . . or at the other extreme, it can almost totally paralyze action.'
Myra Chave-Jones, *Coping with Depression*

'To simplify, . . . the development of a depressive illness depends on two main factors, stress and susceptibility.'
Dr Brice Pitt, *Making the Most of Middle Age*

One of the important lessons that doctors and lay people have been relearning in recent years is that physical health and mental well-being belong together. They cannot be separated. At one time only a few selected diseases were thought to have links with the sufferer's state of mind, but now it is recognized that a whole range — from cancer to heart attack — may be brought on by worry and strain. For that reason alone it is important to come to terms with the factors that are causing anxiety and lack of peace within our minds. It is also important for its own sake. Nothing is worse than feeling screwed up inside or suffering from a sense of utter emptiness and loss of interest or emotion. Two of the main villains of the piece in midlife are tension and depression.

Tension

In her book, *The Prime of Your Life*, Dr Miriam Stoppard writes, 'Living in the twentieth century means that we feel more stress than any members of the human race have ever felt.' But a contemporary writer described life in 1883 as 'this age of stress and transition'. No doubt stress and change have always characterized human society and psychiatrists point out that these two factors are closely linked. Any change in situation can produce stress and that includes happy events, such as getting married or winning the pools. You may have seen a table of life-events which indicates the relative effects of change on stress level. The death of a spouse and loss of job merit the highest stress rating, and the low end of the scale includes holidays and Christmas! When several of these life-events closely follow one another, the level of stress is increased enormously. Considering the number of changes associated with midlife, it is not surprising that stress is especially high at this period.

It is important to recognize that stress is not bad in itself. The physical reactions that stress triggers help us to jump out of the way of a passing bus, or win the egg and spoon race at the village sports day. We all need stress in order to achieve and do our best work. Without it we should not have the motive or stimulus to reach our goals or survive some of the situations in which we find ourselves.

Stress also relieves the tedium of everyday life. Many people doing boring or repetitive jobs deliberately introduce a certain amount of stress to make the routine more exciting. I used to set myself time targets for ironing a certain number of shirts and try to beat previous records in order to give zest to an otherwise monotonous job.

Stress becomes harmful only when it exceeds our ability to cope with the situation, or when it continues unrelieved over a prolonged period. An engineering expert in stress told me that it has recently been discovered that two pieces of metal, indistinguishable unless subjected to sophisticated tests, react differently to precisely the same amount of stress. One piece remains undamaged but the other breaks. In the same way, human beings differ from one another in their ability to handle stress and the level at which they can cope comfortably. Even the same person reacts differently on different occasions, depending on how fit they are and on other circumstances at that time.

Stress may result from a sudden dramatic turn of affairs or a so-called 'life-event', but it is more often largely the result of long-term overwork or anxiety. Years of caring for a sick, disabled or elderly relative, or months of waiting to hear whether a job is to end, cause stress to accumulate in our lives. It is easy to be unaware of the pressures we are under until they have built up to a head. We sometimes surprise ourselves as well as our near and dear ones by suddenly exploding into unreasonable anger over a trifling offence which just happens to be the last straw that breaks the camel's back.

When we feel unwell in some way or another we do not always recognize stress as the culprit. A doctor spoke recently of the many patients who came to him — mostly men — complaining of stiff neck, poor sleep, loss of appetite and failing sexual desire. None spoke of stress but all were suffering from it, and their physical symptoms were the direct result. It can be a relief to discover that some of the worrying physical symptoms are not the first indications of some dreaded disease but are stress-related and represent perfectly normal ways of reacting to stress. But, since too much stress plays a part in causing a number of more serious physical disorders — including heart, breathing, digestive, muscle and mental troubles — it is doubly important to come to grips and control it. Unwanted and harmful stress should not be accepted as an unwelcome but inevitable ingredient of midlife.

Coming to terms with stress

A first step in dealing with unwanted stress could be to write down all the factors which you think may be causing undue stress in your life at present. These may include some major events, such as divorce, moving house, suffering the loss of a loved person, or starting a new job. Over and above such dramatic ingredients of change and stress you probably have a long-term commitment which is stressful too. This may involve caring for someone elderly, or just trying to keep relationships smooth in a house full of teenage sons and daughters. You may suffer from having more to do in twenty-four hours than is humanly possible, or, at the other extreme, find yourself with too little interesting activity to make each day worthwhile.

When you have made your list, try to decide — with the help of someone close and understanding if need be — how you can cut down on the pressures, or alter the circumstances, in order to relieve excess stress. Get your priorities right and whittle away the non-essentials. (For example, the fact that you have always hoovered and polished every week need not mean you must continue to do so.) Plan ahead to relieve periods of special busyness or tension. If there is one day in the week on which you visit your mother-in-law and work an evening shift, don't be tempted to do the week's shopping in a crowded supermarket en route. Try to reserve a small oasis of quietness and time to relax instead. Emotional well-being is even more precious than time.

Wherever possible, share your worries with someone else. At this very busy period of life, get all the help you can. Going it alone is often a matter of pride and does no one a service. If you are working outside as well as inside the home, try to use some of your earnings to ease household jobs — for example, substitute duvets for sheets and blankets to save laundry and bed-making, or buy a food processor to do in seconds what takes hours by hand. If you are looking after an elderly relative, make use of any help groups and agencies that exist to relieve you. See that other members of the family, if you have one, stop depending on you to do everything for them, as they did when they were younger.

If there is still more to fit into a week than is humanly possible, do what a doctor advised me to do. Sort out your priorities by making a list of all your activities and marking those which you — and only you — can do. They may include being a wife to your husband, a mother to your children, or a daughter to your parents. They may also include specific commitments you have taken on, or skills which only you possess. But you may find that some of these skills could be taught to others, so that you are not always responsible for cooking meals, or washing and ironing clothes. There is no reason why the ability to use a washing-machine or a pressure cooker should be limited to one person per household!

Men too may need to learn to delegate duties both at work and at home. Fear of losing our grip may make us hang on to jobs for longer than we should, in an attempt to reassure ourselves.

Give enough time to yourself and your own physical, mental, emotional and spiritual needs. When you are tense it is hard to relax but that is just what you need to do. You may be able to make time to join relaxation classes. If not, there are simple relaxation routines which you can follow for yourself and fit into your daily routine. Deep breathing is a good method of relaxation and so are the 'tense and let go' exercises, in which the muscles of various parts of the body in turn — face, shoulders, hands and so on — are deliberately screwed up tight and then released to achieve complete relaxation. Walking and swimming are also excellent for releasing tension. Some activity that will relax your mind is important too, especially just before bed.

Dr Richard Ecker takes a very different view of stress from most practitioners. In his book, *The Stress Myth*, he contradicts the usual assumption that unwanted stress is an inevitable part of life and teaches that instead of looking for ways of dealing with it after it has occurred, we ourselves should take action to prevent it happening at all. It is not other people or outward events that cause harmful stress, but the way we perceive such external factors and our fears of what they will do to us. Since we cannot control the events of life we must control our responses. Much of the time we are reacting with unwanted stress because we are afraid of doing damage to our own self-concept. For example, as parents we may react with undue stress to a teenager who flouts our authority, because we are afraid of losing our self-esteem which is dependent on being able to control our family.

Dr Ecker concludes that 'the ultimate step in the process of stress prevention is changing the way we view ourselves and our place in the world. If I can make these changes, I can be freed from my captivity to unwanted stress. No longer will I hold on to my lifelong belief that events in the world around me threaten my personal identity. I will understand that my identity in the image of God is secure and that my life has special value. . . I can be certain of who I am, no matter what happens in the world around me.'

The stress and tension that result from anxiety are unnecessary burdens. Jesus taught his followers that life was meant to be lived a day at a time. It would be foolish as well as useless, he said, to worry about how to cope with tomorrow when there is quite enough to cope with today. Anyway, we have in God a loving Father who is both aware of our needs and perfectly able and ready to provide for them. St Paul gave the same excellent advice — 'Don't worry!' But unlike many well-meaning friends, he followed it up with a practical alternative: 'Tell God every detail of your needs in earnest and thankful prayer, and the peace of God, which transcends human under-standing, will keep constant guard over your hearts and minds as they rest in Christ Jesus.' (From Philippians chapter 4, J.B. Phillips' translation.)

Depression

It is a great pity that the same word — depression — is used to describe both the common human experience of Monday morning blues and also a clinically diagnosable illness. Too often, friends and colleagues react to the information that someone is suffering from depression either by agreeing that they often feel a bit down themselves but manage to cope, or else by treating the person as if he or she were suffering from mental disease.

The factors that cause stress can also cause clinical depres-sion and, surprisingly perhaps, as with stress, changes in life which are happy and positive may bring on depression as well as those associated with sadness and loss. The illness may also be connected with hormone imbalance as in post-natal and menopausal depression. Genes seem to enter into it too. Some people have a greater inherited tendency to depression than others. Depression may result from an upbringing which induced feelings of insecurity, inadequacy or false guilt which have dogged the young adult's steps until they finally come to a head during the crisis of midlife. Feelings of anger and bitter-ness towards another person, as well as guilt, which have been pushed down and never dealt with, may also cause depression. Chronic overwork can bring about depression too. Only a quali-fied person can unravel the causes.

Depression may be accompanied by feelings of sadness but more typical symptoms are fear and panic attacks, loss of energy, a general slowing down, even of speech, lack of appe-tite for food, sex or normal interests, inability to concentrate or make decisions, and disturbed sleep patterns. The experience of depression is almost impossible to describe to those who have not suffered from it. It is painful and distressing in the extreme. But there is a way through and in spite of how the sufferer may feel at the time, there will be a return to normality.

Most of us, men especially, do not readily admit to depression. It seems to be an admission of failure and weakness, especially when others are coping perfectly well with what appear to be even greater strains. Sadly, too, psychiatric disorders are still viewed by many people with suspicion and prejudice. But it is very important to get medical help in the early stages. Trying to carry on with the normal routine while suffering from depression has been likened to driving a car in top gear with the brakes full on. Myra Chave-Jones, a psychotherapist, in her book *Coping with Depression* says, 'The successful and lasting treatment of depression involves openly acknowledging its existence. If it is denied or suppressed in some way, it will become a recurring experience, or it will convert itself into some other disorder of the body, emotion or behaviour. Successful treatment includes resolving the conflicts that produce depression — conflicts from within our inner life, or outer circumstances. Then it is likely that when we recover we will not slip back again into that same pit.'

Medical help may take a number of different forms. Antidepressants may be prescribed. These are not tranquillizers and are non-habit-forming. Psychiatrists themselves are not certain exactly how they work but they replace certain amines which appear to be low in those suffering depression. Psychotherapy and group therapy — as an out-patient or in-patient — may also be prescribed. Many people emerge from therapy far better adjusted and able to cope with life than others who have not been compelled by illness to work through loss and learn to know themselves. Therapy often helps people to appraise themselves honestly. They learn their strengths and weaknesses and are sufficiently confident and free to shed the masks that most of us wear in order to hide our inadequacies both from ourselves and from others. In coping with their depression they will also have gained insights that will help them to understand other people better and be more able to offer acceptable sympathy and help.

Those who have a commitment to the Christian faith are not thereby immune from depression. In fact they may bear an added burden of guilt. The Christian life should be one of joy and peace, they feel, so either they have failed God or he has let them down — though they feel guilty for thinking so. One characteristic of depression is to feel utterly alone and bereft of help or hope and it is therefore almost impossible to feel

God's love and nearness at such a time. One Christian therapist believes that much depression can be helped if the patient can separate out the love of God from the love of his or her own father. Parental love may have been conditional, and acceptance dependent on behaving in the 'right' ways. God's love is utterly unconditional and never failing.

One man described his experience of depression in this way: 'Early in the crisis I became deeply aware that God was my ally. I could tell him anything, even share with him the contradictory motives within my personality, and he would still love and accept me. As the crisis deepened and I came into the depression and withdrawal stages, I knew intellectually that God was still my friend, even though I did not feel it emotionally.'

Dr Leslie Weatherhead wrote, in *Prescription for Anxiety*, 'Deadness of feeling, even if we think we do not love anybody, not even God, must not make us worry. Love and trust still exist, but because the emotional machinery that registers them has gone wrong, we do not feel as we used to. But the machinery can, and will, be mended. Moreover, the truth that matters is not what we feel, but the fact that God loves us whatever we feel, and his energies are always tending towards our health and well-being.'

Recognizing what God is really like, and knowing that he is our ally, can point the way back to health and wholeness.

ACTION CHECKPOINTS

☐ Examine sources of stress — reduce causes where possible.

☐ Exercise to reduce tension.

☐ Take early signs of depression seriously — get help.

☐ Make opportunities to relax.

☐ Check your personal basis for self-worth.

6
THE BODY BEAUTIFUL

The Things People Say

'There is no reason to think your looks will fade just because you have reached the menopause. You can go on feeling lively and young and be as sexually attractive as you want, so long as you take care of your health.'
Dr Jean Coope, *The Menopause*

'One should not complain that people are keeping their looks. . . longer than they ever have before. But what worries me is that, since middle age has been put to flight, will old age descend overnight like a sudden frost on the dew?'
Penny Perrick, journalist

'Our outward appearance undoubtedly alters as we get older and for most people the condition of the skin and hair is the final arbiter of age.'
Dr Miriam Stoppard, *The Prime of Your Life*

'The most significant factor about the baby-boomers has been their reluctance to give up their youthfulness. They've introduced diet consciousness and the whole "looking good" thing. They've been responsible for making Joan Collins a sex symbol at fifty-three. A forty-year-old today looks a lot better than a forty-year-old of twenty years ago.'
John Perris of Saatchi and Saatchi, quoted by Steve Turner in *The Times*

'When taking a fresh look at your wardrobe, editing it to suit your lifestyle, don't neglect to amass a good accessory selection.'
Fashion editor, advising older women

'Growing older may mean you have to work harder to stay in shape, but it can be done — think of all the glamorous film stars who are in their fifties!'
Living with the Menopause

'The more readily someone agrees to grow old, the younger they seem to be.'
Ronald Eyre, television presenter

Most of us would pay lip service to the message of chapter 3, that the clue to true beauty is to be found in personality and character. A beauty that springs from inward tranquillity and an unselfconscious concern for others contributes to the kind of beauty that will outlast youth. Good nature and a sense of humour, as well as an alert and well-stocked mind are also reflected in the face. We recognize, too, that a healthy lifestyle contributes more to looking good than skilfully used cosmetics. Keeping weight down, getting exercise and eating the right foods are important to beauty as well as health. Many of the health tips in chapters 4 and 5 are beauty tips too. Eating the right kind of food and having a balanced diet is important not only for weight control but for the well-being of skin, hair and every other part of us that we tend to treat in terms of beauty rather than health care.

In spite of acknowledging all these factors, most of us still spend an inordinate amount of time prettifying and refurbishing the outside of ourselves. After all, that is the first thing about us that others see and a well-groomed, well-dressed image reflected back at us from the mirror goes a long way to bolstering our private and public confidence. Magazine articles, in an attempt to help us improve that image, advise us to stand sideways on, without our clothes, before a long mirror, and check up honestly on our general shape. That's fine, for those with the courage to do it, but most of us have enough shocks in midlife when we catch sight of ourselves fully cloth-ed. An accidental glimpse in a shop window or mirror may bring us up with a jolt. For a split second, I have sometimes failed to recognize that it is my own face that is being reflected back at me. I had not realized that I looked so old and tired.

How are we going to come to terms with the ageing process, once we notice it? Are we going to hide the ravages of time as cleverly as we can for a few more years, or gradually make the necessary adaptations in order to create a new image that is not a faded version of the old but corresponds in an attractive and lively way to the new stage in life which we have reached? Our response to this question probably reflects our overall reaction to reaching midlife.

We all gladly agree that today most people of forty — or even fifty for that matter — look as if they are still in their thirties. The Joan Collins syndrome is one way of summing up the present attempt to take ten to fifteen years off the way women look. Perhaps, instead of seeing the whole operation as a put-up job, we ought to accept a changed concept of what a fifty-year-old looks like. Such shifts in perception keep recurring.

In Victorian and post-Victorian times, a woman of forty might settle down to wearing black and being an old lady. Queen Victoria, in her widow's weeds, provided that kind of model. But at that time, too, women who reached their mid-forties were frequently exhausted by constant child-bearing and hard physical work. Even forty or fifty years ago, middle age arrived in the forties, at which time it was normal to develop a comfortable middle-aged spread and to withdraw from the sex and beauty stakes.

Women today have the chance to stay looking young for longer. Their general health is better and they do not suffer repeated or unwanted pregnancies as a matter of course. Easy-to-run homes and a host of electrical aids mean that heavy housework does not take the toll it once did.

Looking young is important to many women today in order to hold their own with confidence in the world outside the home, whether they are married or single. Sad to say, in some fields of work looking middle-aged can be a definite disadvantage. The media confirm that impression. Very few middle-aged women, if any, present television news or programmes. Jobs apart, looking young and sexy may still seem important and desirable to many of those who have grown up in a society which lays such emphasis on youth and sex.

There is another reason for retaining a younger image at forty and fifty than our mothers or grandmothers did. After all, now that women in particular live longer, middle age might be assumed to begin a few years later too. The difficulty lies in the fact that the edges are blurred and no one is sure just when youth may be said to be past and the second stage of adult life begun.

The important thing to sort when we pass the forty mark is the motive that lies behind the wish to stay looking young. If we believe that it is right to push back the boundaries of middle age a few years, we can happily keep our young tastes and looks for a bit longer. But if we go on refusing to accept our true age and try instead to remain at a stage of life to which we no longer properly belong, then looking younger than our years is a false statement. Refusing to come to terms with reality harms us and, incidentally, deceives no one else for long.

One test of our response to the change made by age is what we decide to do about grey hair. Many women who go grey early maintain the looks that belong to their real age by having their hair colour-rinsed. But if we go grey within the normal range of time our reaction may be an indicator of our overall attitude to the whole effect of ageing on our looks. Sophisticated dyes and colourings make it possible to hide this sign of age for as long as we wish and those in public life may, unfortunately, believe that only by covering the tell-tale grey will they maintain their credibility as energetic and creative top people. For the rest of us, coming to terms with our grey hair and living with it may be a practical way of encouraging us to come to terms with our chronological age and of easing ourselves into a new age group. Midlife is an important and exciting time which has no need to borrow the outgrown trappings of youth.

'Be your age' is not advice to look dowdy, dull and unattractive, but a directive to discover the good looks and beauty that are proper to the new stage of life. There is all the difference between keeping slim, well-groomed and well-dressed in order to look good at forty-five or fifty, and putting the same amount of effort into an attempt to put back the clock and have another crack at being twenty-five.

All the same, in order to look good as well as feel good, men and women over forty need to take extra care to overcome the outward effects of wear and tear on most parts of the body.

Looking tired

Many years ago there was an advertisement which showed a couple dressed for an evening out, with the caption, '"You look tired," he said, and spoilt her evening.' My mother used to say that if anyone told her she was looking tired, she knew it meant that she was not looking very attractive either. Many people at midlife find it incredibly hard to get time to sit down, let alone spend an extra hour in bed. But ten minutes spent relaxing flat on the floor, or comfortably seated in a darkened room, can do wonders to replenish energies as well as looks. Keeping on the go can become a habit and there are very many people who could manage to let up for ten minutes or more in the course of most days, with a bit of careful planning.

Skin

Skin becomes drier as we grow older. Those with oily or normal complexions may need to change the kind of face creams used and those whose skins have always been dry will need to take even more care and possibly change to a heavier cream. It is important to use moisturizing cream day and night so that the skin should feel soft as well as looking good.

Manufacturers are happy to exploit what is often a more affluent age-group, in order to launch anti-wrinkle preparations and other seemingly magic preparations for the 'mature' skin. But there is probably no substance that will make wrinkles disappear permanently and by midlife many of the lines on our faces have been etched there by laughter or frowns over the years.

It is possible to pay the earth for beauty products. The packaging and product name usually make up a hefty part of that cost. Some people find it does them good psychologically to use an expensive preparation but it is possible to keep the skin soft and free from unpleasant dryness without spending a fortune. Inexpensive, non-perfumed creams will relieve dry skin on hands and feet as well as face. Men as well as women may need to use such a cream. Geoffrey Aquilina Ross, in *How to Survive the Male Menopause*, recommends a quick night-time routine for face and neck, which even tired and busy people can manage. It should include:

- Cleansing (with cleansing cream or good, unperfumed soap, such as oatmeal, and warm, not hot, water)

- Toning with an astringent

- Moisturizing with your chosen cream

Make-up requirements may change, as skin tones and hair colour change too. Most people prefer the total look to be soft and natural without some of the extravagances and hard colours of younger-style make-up, but that is partly a matter of personal taste and overall style.

Hands and feet as well as face and neck may suffer from dryness and need a similar moisturizing cream at night. Keep some hand cream near the kitchen sink as well as the bathroom basin, so that a dab is put on whenever hands have been in water. Some hand creams care for nails at the same time. For most busy people a bath is not a long-drawn-out luxury (even getting into the bathroom may be a problem when there are teenagers around). But the occasional bath with bath oil and a relaxed soak, followed by body lotion lovingly applied, can do great things for the morale and help the appearance too.

Feet

By midlife more than a nightly application of cream may be needed to keep feet happy and comfortable. Women tend to have more foot problems than men from years of wearing fashion shoes. When the feet are hurting it shows in the face, as well as making you thoroughly miserable, so go to see a qualified chiropodist. When it's a do-it-yourself job, remember always to cut nails straight across. Make sure that stockings or tights as well as shoes are not too tight. Frequent washing and thorough drying of feet makes them feel comfortable and keeps them healthy.

Eyes

Vision changes at around forty, so a visit to an ophthalmic optician is important. They are qualified not only to check whether you need glasses but also to spot early signs of any serious eye troubles, as well as some other kinds of disease, and to recommend referral to a specialist when necessary. Many people wear contact lenses. If you wear glasses full-time, you should take trouble over selecting frames. You will wear them more frequently than any single outfit of clothes and it is worth paying as much as you can afford to get a pair that make you feel and look good. Don't be persuaded to be safe and sensible when you would rather be dashing and adventurous in your choice.

Teeth

Dental health is an important ingredient of total physical fitness. It also has a good deal to do with how we look. After teenage years, the most common cause of tooth loss is gum disease, so regular brushing should include gums as well as teeth. Sweet things should be an after-meal treat only. Regular visits to the dentist are still important. Those who have lost their teeth and wear dentures should still visit their dentist every six months. Ideally, dentures should be renewed every three or four years. Clean dentures with a soft brush and soap and water after every meal and leave them in water overnight.

Hair

What you do about grey hairs has already been discussed. Apart from that, in midlife as at every age, a good cut — about once every six weeks — is the single most important way to keep hair looking good, with an occasional soft perm or demi wave, when required. Cleanliness is very important for hair as for every other part of the body. Hair sometimes changes from being dry to becoming greasy at this age but as likely as not will revert later to its usual condition. Baby shampoo is excellent — and cheap — for fine or out of condition hair.

- Massage the scalp gently before washing.

- Use tepid water.

- Make one application of shampoo only.

- Rinse thoroughly.

- Towel dry gently.

- Avoid using hot dryer whenever possible.

Geoffrey Ross comments, 'It has been noticed that many men wash their hair in water that is too hot (which over-stimulates the sebaceous glands and so makes the scalp greasier than it should be) and are rough-actioned with the towel when drying the hair. This may seem a macho way to treat the hair but it is also a sure way for pulling the hair out. So too is brushing. Never use a brush. For tidying the hair use a wide-toothed comb.'

The total look

Getting your act together successfully also depends on the clothes you wear. A man's advice to men at midlife is neither to try dressing like younger men nor to neglect the way they dress. In brief: take time and shop around for clothes that are adventurous but classic. Buy less but spend more — not on expensive designer clothes intended for the young, but on well-cut quality clothes. Avoid strong primaries as well as dull colours like lovat. Keep clothes scrupulously clean and well-cared for.

In spite of a wardrobe bulging with clothes, most women complain that they haven't a thing to wear when any invitation arrives in the post. A leading fashion editor suggests that in fact we have too many, rather than too few, clothes. Her first bit of advice, especially to older women, is to go through the wardrobe, ruthlessly discarding anything that no longer fits, no longer looks good on us, or has long since seen better days.

Anyone who has had the courage to do that is ready for the next stage. Resist the temptation to buy on impulse, just because an outfit catches the eye. That, it seems, is what most of us tend to do. Instead, wardrobes should be planned seriously and with proper care.

First decide on your own lifestyle and the kind of clothes that you need. Be prepared to buy fewer but better clothes. Choose one or two basic colours for major items and introduce other shades for smaller items, such as knitwear and accessories. This plan of campaign gives scope for far more variety and flexibility. The right fashionable scarf, belt, necklace, etc. can be used simply and quickly to update outfits and add variety to simple clothes. These days there is a wide price range available in co-ordinated outfits, both in chain stores and in the well-known brand-name clothes to be found in department stores, so nearly everyone can afford to look and feel good. Clothes that suit teenagers may no longer suit the forty-five-year-old, but she, in turn, is able to carry off fashions that youngsters would not have the poise or elegance to wear.

Every age has its own beauty. The skill in midlife is to discover the beauty that belongs to that stage in life and to accept it willingly. Those who make the most of their new image in a positive and welcoming way will feel good and look good too.

ACTION CHECKPOINTS

☐ Visit the dentist/optician/chiropodist.

☐ Begin new skin care routine if necessary.

☐ Rethink hair care and styling.

☐ Eat to look good.

☐ Watch weight.

☐ Get enough exercise.

☐ Get enough rest and sleep.

☐ Check present wardrobe and rethink approach to dress.

SECTION 3
THE OLDER GENERATION

7

TENDER LOVING CARE

The Things People Say

'A grandmother is a lady who has no children of her own, so she likes other people's little girls and boys. A grandfather is a man grandmother. He goes for walks with the boys and they talk about fishing and tractors.'
Eight-year-old girl

'A harmonious intimacy between grandparents and grandchildren can very often be an incomparably precious blessing to both.'
Dr Paul Tournier, psychiatrist and author

'Both grannies are very different. I suppose they get on reasonably well, but they do tend to rub each other up. And I'm pig in the middle.'
Forty-five-year-old housewife

'I do not think that a single relative should ever have the sole care of a senile dependent. Two people are needed to share the load.'
Daughter who cared for her father

'Carers tend to feel guilty and often have too little compassion for themselves. They need support.'
Spokesperson from the National Council for Carers

'The caring situation can prove very frustrating both from the social and the job opportunity points of view. And some carers and dependents find it difficult to adapt to a role reversal — the old person of course not wanting to relinquish her dominant role and the carer finding it difficult to cope with becoming the decision maker.'
Report by the National Council for Carers

Many adults survive the stormy family period of adolescence and go on to form happy and close relationships with their parents. There seems to be far more scope at the present time for the two generations to become friends. The authoritarian parent or dutiful child attitudes that so often characterized these relationships in previous generations are thankfully on the way out. Today's senior citizens may complain that they do not receive the respect or consideration that was expected from them by their parents, but most of them welcome the far more open and equal relationship which exist between them and their adult children.

The new relationship combines the pleasure of intimate friendship with the added benefits of a close and shared past. Wise parents are still able to give support and advice, when it is asked for, even after their children have set up their own homes or married and had a family. Frequent visits, long telephone calls and letters, all keep the links strong. And the parents often benefit as much from the acquired wisdom and expertise of their children as the children do from theirs. There is mutual respect and affection. Not all who reach midlife have parents still living, and those who do may not be on such happy terms with them. But plenty are, and both parents and children find great strength and satisfaction from the relationship.

Those with children of their own can also gain enormously from the part that their parents play as grandparents. Some live too far away to be closely involved in the day-to-day happenings of the younger generation, but visits to Granny and Grandpa, accompanied by the family or as special guests on their own, can be important highlights in a child's life.

At the other extreme, some grandparents are forced by cir- cumstances, or by their children's choices, to behave as sub- stitute mothers and fathers. Ideally — emergencies apart — grandparents should not be fretted and concerned with the day-in and day-out duties of child-rearing. They have already done their turn at this. As grandparents they should be free to be detached, and to give time and care of a different and spe- cial kind, which harassed and busy parents are often not able to provide. As an eight-year-old explained:

'Grandmothers don't have to do anything but be there. They are old so they shouldn't play hard or run. They should never say, "Hurry up". Usually they are fat, but not too fat to tie children's shoes. . . They don't have to be smart, only answer questions, like why dogs hate cats and why God isn't married. . . When they read to us they don't skip bits, or mind if it is the same story over again. Every- body should have one, especially if you don't have television, because grandmothers are the only grown-ups who have the time!'

Grandparents don't only give their grandchildren time. They are also able to give them individual understanding, recognizing the uniqueness and importance of each grandchild. Every human being feels the need to receive this kind of attention from someone close and caring. Grandparents can be of special help to a child who feels — mistakenly or not — that he or she is the odd one out or a failure compared to the others in the family. They may invite one child at a time to come to visit or stay, and give each the luxury of being an 'only' for a little while.

Dr Paul Tournier, the Swiss psychiatrist, wrote about a grandmother's influence on his own wife. When they became engaged, his future mother-in-law said about her daughter, 'I hope you will understand her. I never have.' But her *grandmother* had. When she was a child, she had invited her to stay. She had encouraged her and taken an interest in her special aptitudes and gifts. Dr Tournier comments: 'It is true that grandparents can often understand their children better than the parents do, and give them the acceptance they need in order to grow up.'

The bond between grandparents and grandchildren can remain strong during the difficult years of adolescence. My own mother died when our daughter was eighteen. I had not realized how close they had been but she grieved for a long while for the grandmother to whom she had felt close and in whom she had found it easy to confide.

Obviously, not all families live in such close and happy relationships, with each generation fulfilling its distinctive role. Family breakdown is common and there are a large number of single parent families, with the result that many grandparents share in or take over the upbringing of their grandchildren and behave as parents to them. At the other extreme, there are many who have lost contact almost completely with their grandchildren following the death, or divorce and remarriage, of one of the parents.

Role change

Sadly, the time comes when fit, able-bodied older people begin to lose their health and strength. The decline may sometimes be very gradual but in other cases a heart attack or stroke makes an immediate change in lifestyle necessary. The decline may be mental, as with the onset of Altzheimer's disease (senile dementia), or a progressive disease of the central nervous system which may or may not involve mental deterioration. Some people's behaviour changes after they have suffered a stroke. Quite apart from the practical problems of care, the family is faced with the sadness of coming to terms with change in a person they have known and probably loved all their life. As well as feeling a sense of sadness and loss, the son or daughter begins to realize that the parent is now depending on them for strength and care.

One middle-aged daughter put it this way: 'I suddenly realized that my mother and I had changed roles. I had relied on her for support of every kind, long after I was grown-up. Now she was relying on me.'

It is hard, after a lifetime of sharing disappointments and problems with a parent, to find that they are no longer capable of sustaining conversation, that their memory is failing or that they have little interest in things outside their own immediate situation. Instead of sharing burdens they must be protected from anxiety, and their worries and fears allayed. Coming to terms mentally and emotionally with such change in an elderly relative is as much part of coping with the situation as providing the practical care that they need.

At the receiving end

Elderly parents also have to grapple with a change in role. Those who are mentally alert may not find it easy or pleasant to take help from the very ones they have supported and cared for over the years. Many parents dread the thought of having to depend on their children. It is extremely painful for them to add to their burdens at a time when they are most hard pressed at work or with their own families. Busy carers may make good provision for the physical needs of the parent without considering how they must be feeling.

Older people who have lived full and interesting lives will feel the loss of stimulus once they are housebound. One woman, who took up a new career in midlife, described how her mother, who had always had a great appetite for life, now seemed to live through her. She took such an avid interest in all that her daughter was doing that it became stressful. But such intense interest can work to the carer's advantage too.

Another older woman, who had lived alone with her mother since her father died, recalled the satisfaction of coming home to someone with all the time in the world to listen to what she had to tell about her day in the office or an evening at choir practice. Now that her mother has died, she sadly misses the interest and advice that was always forthcoming. Many of us have valued the interest focussed on our needs and problems by a parent who was physically disabled but mentally alert and concerned. Others overlook this opportunity to share their interests with parents and don't even seem aware of their parents' need for mental and emotional stimulus.

Someone described seeing a couple having tea in a restaurant with an elderly parent. Husband and wife kept up their own conversation, turning to the elderly lady from time to time only to offer her another cup of tea or a cake. They no doubt thought that they were fulfilling their filial duty by providing her with an outing and 'treat'.

What kind of care?
Sooner or later it may become impossible for an elderly person or couple to continue living in their own home without support. There are various pointers that help us to decide when that time has come. They include:

- badly failing sight

- frequent falls

- loss of memory

- disablement through arthritis, Parkinson's disease, etc.

- severe heart problems

- stroke and disabling after-effects

- senile dementia

When the doctor confirms that it is important to provide care, or when too much anxiety is felt in leaving an elderly person alone, the time has come to consider alternative options. It is important to weigh up all possible courses of action, and the factors for and against, before making a decision that cannot easily be reversed. Here are some of the choices on offer:

● **A home with one or other of the 'children'.** In ideal circumstances a son or daughter may be able to provide a granny flat or at least a bedsitting-room which the older person can call their own and where they can have some personal furniture and possessions as well as privacy. Often it is not possible to provide any separate accommodation at all and even the bedroom may have to be shared. One friend of mine had her mother-in-law living with them from their wedding day. When I knew her, some years ago, their teenage daughter was having to share a bedroom with her granny. Such an arrangement would probably be considered out of the question today, and rightly so.

Whatever the arrangements, it is very important to get ground rules agreed before the move takes place, so that some of the possible snags for all concerned are foreseen and nipped in the bud. When an extended family is living together at close quarters, even minor irritations can grow out of all proportion. One friend, whose widowed father has come to share their home, told me how hard it is to put up with his constant smoking. Theirs had always been a smoke-free household. Yet she hadn't the heart to forbid him to smoke when he had so few comforts left.

In many cases, it may be a matter of giving ground, out of kindness and consideration for the older person, who has been stripped of so much already. Someone else told me of a friend who brought her ninety-year-old mother to visit her. The elderly lady found a private moment in which to invite her hostess to come to see her in the room she occupied in her daughter's house. She explained that she was often lonely, living in a new district, but did not want to interfere with the family, who had their own lives to lead.

• **An easily run home of their own, near to one of the family**. One hindrance to this arrangement may be the old person's unwillingness to move away from their own circle of friends and familiar places. The fact that many people of working age face constant moves to other areas may also complicate the decision. But where the scheme is feasible it can relieve the pressures for all concerned. There is still likely to be a considerable extra work load for the daughter or daughter-in-law who is likely to bear the brunt of extra shopping, washing and keeping an eye on the elderly people.

One friend, who has a job as well as a family of five, has her widowed mother living round one corner and her mother-in-law round the other. Her mother is fairly fit but still finding it difficult to come to terms with her husband's death. Her mother-in-law is blind and becoming very forgetful, but is still unwilling to come to live with them. Somehow, both mothers have to be visited, cared for and made to feel wanted. If the grandchildren visit one granny, they must make sure to visit the other one too. The strains are emotional as much as physical, as the carer tries to keep everyone happy as well as trying to make sure, as far as possible, that no harm befalls the elderly mothers during the hours that they spend on their own.

Another friend, whose husband is a farmer, shares the care of her parents, who live in a neighbouring village, with a married sister, who also lives nearby. Between them they give their mother the support she needs since their father has had a stroke. But her mother is always distressed when she leaves, and dismayed that she has to go before doing just one more job to help. Fortunately, a brother and his wife take responsibility at nights, when the mother will often ring for reassurance about her husband. Many people are in this situation of trying to find time to care adequately for parents in their own home, while running their own jobs and family.

It is hard to offer solutions. Perhaps it helps to explain to parents beforehand what time is available for visits and to stick to those limits as a general rule. The quality of care given during the visits matters more than the actual time spent with them. To be able to give parents all our attention while we are with them, and to shed other responsibilities during that period, may be more help than longer visits undertaken in a hurried and half-attentive way.

● **Sheltered accommodation**. This is probably one of the most attractive solutions on offer for those still able to manage without full-time care. There are many housing schemes which provide small apartments or flats — both 'single' and 'double' size — under the care of a warden, who checks regularly that the residents are safe and well. There is a communicating alarm system from the flats to the warden's office. The residents have their own furniture and are self-sufficient, although there is often a meals' scheme as well as a communal laundry. Sometimes an additional flat is vacant for visiting family or friends from a distance who wish to stay overnight. In many cases such housing provides the best combination of privacy and adequate care. People in their sixties who are on their own are also beginning to move into such accommodation, giving a good mix of younger, able-bodied and older residents.

● **Residential care**. State-provided homes are suitable for those not able to care for themselves. They are usually purpose-built, with facilities to help disabled peopl,e and are staffed by qualified people. They are usually of a high standard. For some alert inmates, there may be too little stimulus in mixing only with others who are extremely old or senile.

Standards vary enormously in privately run old people's homes and nursing homes. There are guide-lines on standards of care but these are not always adhered to even when charges are high. Some are excellent but it is very important to check thoroughly and to be completely satisfied about patient care and the right kind of atmosphere before making definite arrangements.

● **Hospital geriatric ward**. It is not the aim to keep elderly people long-term in such wards. Beds are usually occupied by psycho-geriatrics.

● **Remaining in their own home with carer living in**. Many daughters, and even sons, who are unmarried, or who have returned to their parents' home after a marriage breakdown, may find themselves, in process of time, caring for their elderly parents. Sometimes a single son or daughter will give up their own home to come back and care for parents. Sometimes the carer will not move in completely. I knew a family of five devoted daughters — all married — who took it in turns, when their father died, to stay with their widowed mother night and day, on a rota basis, for the years until she died, because they knew that she would not want to leave her own home.

Making the choice

Everyone in the family should be involved in reaching a decision about the care of an elderly relative, and that includes the elderly person concerned. It is important that no decision is taken without thorough investigation of all the possibilities, and that everyone is satisfied that the decision taken is the best all-round solution.

Sometimes members of a family look for something that is convenient to them or that will solve their own feelings of guilt, rather than giving weight to the elderly person's own strong preferences. It can be more difficult when an elderly couple differ themselves as to what they wish to do, or if members of the family disagree. So many mixed feelings of guilt and anxiety, love and hate can blur the issue that it may be important to adopt the suggestion of one therapist and discuss all the issues with a wise counsellor, perhaps a minister or some other friend of the family, who knows most of the people concerned but has none of the strong emotional involvement of a family member. Such a person is detached enough to think clearly and to advise without bias.

Sociologists and doctors agree that to uproot an old person may cause severe trauma. One doctor concluded, 'Compulsory and unprepared transplantation of an aged person is harmful, often fatal.' For this reason, many recommend care at home, if local nursing and social services can give enough back-up help to make it possible. All too often, the facilities are not available. But it is well worth exploring the possibility as provision of care varies, depending on local resources.

Who will do the caring?

The dilemma of who will care for the elderly is greater today than in previous generations. There are now far more people surviving into old age and, since families are smaller, they have fewer children to care for them. Hardly any have unmarried daughters, who in the past were most often expected to do the caring. It is still nearly always a daughter or daughter-in-law who becomes the carer. Statistics show that three out of four carers are women — and most of the remaining twenty-five per cent who are men are caring for a wife rather than a parent. Some single men do care for parents and their lot can be very difficult. The majority of carers are between the ages of forty and sixty, with some eight per cent under forty. In Britain it is estimated that eighty-three per cent of these carers have no outside help whatsoever. Yet caring for a parent coincides with some of the busiest years of life.

Even twenty or thirty years ago single daughters normally cared for elderly parents. The majority of present-day carers are married, although many in this bracket are living alone and supporting themselves and possibly a family too. If there is a single sister, there is no reason why it should be taken for granted that she should shoulder the caring. A married sister may plead that she has a husband and family to look after but that very fact also means that caring will restrict her less. At least she has her family for support and company, and losing some of her friends and social outlets might be less damaging to her than to her single sister. Even when one member of the family takes on the lion's share of caring, there is no reason why brothers and sisters should not make some contribution. It is far better to work out what help each can provide from the start than for one member of the family to be seriously overburdened or feel permanently aggrieved. It is also wiser that the elderly person should grow used to receiving care from several different people before it becomes hard for a sole carer ever to have time off.

Why care?

Taking on the care of an elderly relative is likely to have far-reaching and sometimes long-term effects on the lives of the carer and their family and friends. At the most it may mean giving up a job. At the least it will impose new responsibilities and personal restrictions as well as further demands on time and physical energy. So it is important not to drift into caring or be hustled into it but to think through personal motives for taking it on.

There are three main reasons for taking care of an elderly person. The first and best is because you want to. A great many people love their elderly parent or aunt sufficiently to want to look after them.

Others, who may not have had such a happy relationship with their parents in the past, take on care out of a sense of duty. If this is your motive it is important to recognize it, and to make sure that does not impose too great a burden on the person cared for as well as on yourself. When we feel resentment or act out of a sense of duty it can sometimes be seen and felt by the person concerned.

A third group of carers take on the job because they feel that they have to. Either there is no one else to step in, or doctors and social workers — themselves at their wits' end to find facilities — conspire to bring it about by assuming that such care will be given, for example when a patient is discharged from hospital following a stroke. The professionals concerned do not always ask the carer if she is willing to cope, because they are afraid that she will refuse. They know that there are no alternatives they can suggest because of the lack of local resources.

It is difficult but very important to resist pressure of this kind. In some cases it may be necessary to refuse outright. There are some situations where the relationship between parent and daughter would make intimate care impossible to give, for example where a daughter had been abused by her father as a child. Those who feel able to give a certain amount of care should sort out with doctors and social workers the conditions on which they feel able to offer it, and the extent of care they can give, before they accept responsibility.

If you find yourself in this situation it is important to decide realistically how much you can do and to mark out these boundaries beforehand. When a relationship has never been easy between a parent and child, it is not likely to improve at this stage. You may have physical limitations yourself which would make lifting and other care of a disabled person difficult or impossible. If local services can promise relief of one kind or another, you may be able to undertake the care, make a better job of it and still save local services some money.

There are various ways in which the burden of care can be relieved. You may say, 'Yes, I will take on the caring but I must have a break every six months,' or 'I can only do so if I can be sure that the incontinence service will be reliable.' It is important, too, to set clear limits to how long you can continue caring if the health of the elderly person is likely to deteriorate seriously. It is in the interests of the local services that elderly people should be cared for at home, so the professionals concerned should be asked to give home carers all the help to which they are entitled.

These are some of the questions carers should ask the doctor and social worker:

- How long will I have to care?

- Will I have enough money?

- Will I get any training?

- What about transport?

No one is likely to offer answers unless the questions are directly asked, but there are people who can give the information you need.

Taking the strain

It is important to know what help is forthcoming for you or for the elderly person for whom you are caring. Help may come in many forms, from the provision of a hand rail for the bath to time at a day centre.

However strong and loving the bond between carer and dependant may be, constant long-term caring is likely to bring some frustrations and difficulties. No one knows how long the situation will continue. Caring for an elderly person is an open-ended project. Both single people and married couples may feel a sense of frustration as the years in which they had planned to be more free to go out and about, and less restricted financially, are circumscribed by the demands of caring.

There may be sadness as well as frustration in watching an older person deteriorate mentally. Compassion does not guarantee unlimited patience. Having to repeat things constantly, as well as to listen to the same comments over and over again, can tax the patience of all but a saint. When irritation does spill over, there is a feeling of guilt. It is important that love and forgiveness are still shared, that tenderness is shown and that constant healing follows understandable outbursts on both sides.

Those with experience stress how important it is that the carer and the dependant should not become indispensable to each other or never spend time apart. This is especially important in the case of a carer living alone with the elderly person. Each can become unhealthily dependent on the other. If you are in this situation and have a friend who will come in for an evening so that you can go out, accept their offer for both your sakes. There may be complaints and accusations of neglect to be endured at first, but it is stimulating for the old person to have new company and most important for you, the carer, to maintain some friends and some life outside the home, both for present needs and for the future when you will be alone.

Rewards and satisfactions

Growing old seems to bring a person's true character into stronger relief. Old people as a group are neither sweet nor cross-grained, but each is the sum of the years that lie behind them. We reap what we sow, and others close to us reap the results too. Many adult children gain great happiness from caring for a much-loved parent in the closing years of their life. They learn much from their wisdom and their example. Teenagers can gain, too, as they help care for their grandparents.

There are ways of turning the restrictions and limitations that caring involves into assets. A few months ago a newspaper carried the story of a couple who had created a garden — now to be opened to the public — during the years that they were housebound, caring for sick relatives. They had made this 'botanical extravaganza', with sunken gardens and rhododendrons, out of a plot forty-five by seventy-six feet, in a London suburb, to provide a place of rest. There must be many other ways of capitalizing in a creative way on the restrictions of being housebound.

Men and women at midlife are the generation in the middle. They are concerned with giving both to the younger ones coming up behind them and the older ones ahead, who are nearing the end of life. A man in his forties commented: 'Those in their forties and fifties are the bridge generation, looked to by both younger and older people for mature guidance and help. This is the generation who can hold society together. This is where leadership comes from.'

The scope for bringing influence to bear and exerting power, in the best sense of the word, is probably greater at midlife than at any other time. Most of the time the 'vocation' will be seen as a matter of washing, cleaning, feeding and earning. But to provide security, comfort and a sense of worth to the parents and relatives who belong to us is a job worth doing and worth doing with all the compassion and love that we can give.

ACTION CHECKPOINTS

☐ Foster good relationships with parents.

☐ Where possible, encourage opportunities for grandparents and grandchildren to be together.

When parents need care:

☐ Think through choices carefully.

☐ Consult with all the family.

☐ Seek the advice of a trusted friend if necessary.

☐ Think through the commitment of being a full-time carer beforehand.

☐ Find out about all the help available.

8
THE END OF THE ROAD

The Things People Say

'I went through a period of seeing myself dead, seeing myself in a coffin and the people at my funeral. I imagined it as clearly as one could, to the point where I was ready to go out and buy my burial outfit.'
Thirty-eight-year-old American woman, after the death of her father
(in *Passages* by Gail Sheehy)

'The elderly parent reflects the very fear which the midlife person feels. They present an image of the loss of power, the nearness of old age and, behind it all, the fear of death.'
Bishop Jim Thompson, *Half Way*

Extracts from conversations and letters:

'It was a lovely way for her to go, and we do feel thankful that she didn't linger on and suffer.'

'I suppose my feelings about my father's death were charged with guilt. He ought not to have died, and if I had gone with my mother to the doctor and done my part as a son, I feel as if he need not have done.'

'I suppose all the sorting out at the flat will take up the spare time for quite a while. I'm rather dreading that, but everyone has the problem some time, don't they?'

'I still do miss her so much, but when I'm down I think of the way she kept so cheerful after losing Dad, although she missed him terribly. . . so I try to keep cheerful for her.'

'I cannot express in words the love and care which has been shown to me by all my Christian friends since Mam died.'

'It's a relief to wake up in the middle of the night and to know that Dad is not suffering any longer.'

Both men and women live longer nowadays but, even so, quite a large number of people are going to experience the death of one or both parents when they themselves are reaching midlife. The loss of parents brings with it a whole range of mixed emotions. At the time, these can be difficult to cope with and almost impossible to sort out. Later, it is important to try to understand and work through the different strands of feeling which go to make up the total experience of loss.

Those who have been living near to parents or who have remained in very close touch with them, are going to feel the immediate absence of the parent they loved more keenly than those who have broken away from close family ties and kept up only a dutiful contact with father or mother. But even where there may seem to have been little affection shown and where few apparent links remain, emotional ties that go back to earliest days are strong, and feelings about the death of a parent are bound to go deep.

Immediate reactions

Not everyone reacts to the death of someone close by bursting into tears and behaving in the kind of way that we expect from people experiencing grief. They are more likely to be unable to register any emotion. They may be unable to take in the reality of what has happened. One man, who appeared to have understood and accepted the fact of his mother's death, still got ready to visit her in hospital that evening. The human mind possesses a special mechanism to shut off feelings of overpowering grief, leaving the bereaved person in a state of numbness and shock, until they are ready to cope with what has happened.

During this period of numbness, people are perfectly able to carry on with the practicalities of living. Quite often, a son or daughter will be responsible for the formalities and requirements that follow a death. It may be their first experience of death at close quarters and they will be surprised at how much there is to do. The death certificate may need to be collected from the hospital, the death must be registered, friends and relatives must be informed and the funeral arranged. The right authorities must be informed about pensions and allowances. If the other parent is still living, they must be cared for too. They may want you to help to sort out the personal belongings of the dead partner, which is always a painful job. Above all, they will need your loving understanding and support for some time to come.

Experiencing grief

Grief at the death of parents can take many forms. One woman described how differently she reacted to her father's death, when she was thirty-four, and her mother's death, ten years later:

'When my father died, after a long illness, I was devastated. I managed to leave the children and travel straight to my mother's to help her make all the arrangements. I remember sorting through all his clothes. It was seeing his glasses that tore me apart. I went straight out to the bin to get rid of them before my mother could see them. I felt physically sick all the time and unable to eat but I was able to keep going. Then, when the funeral was over and I was on my way home, I felt really ill. All that summer I was ill — they said they thought it was glandular fever — but I know it was my way of reacting to my father's death. I couldn't even manage the children — friends took them for odd days. I remember not being able to face certain people for months afterwards. I was at a concert with the children a month or so later and saw one rather pushy friend, who I could normally handle. But I just fled rather than talk to her. I had adored my father and I took ages to get over it.

'I reacted quite differently when my mother died. I couldn't understand it. I had loved her dearly and I felt worried that I wasn't feeling the way I had when my father died. I can remember having a really happy time with other relatives after her funeral. But I still have a cry, sometimes, when I realize that my mother is dead — and that's years after. I almost feel as if I have gone on getting to know and understand her after she died, and have done my mourning as I go, whereas with my father the relationship was perfect and complete and ended with his death.'

Sometimes a parent has suffered an illness that has caused mental change or changes in personality, and the family has already gone through much of the bereavement process beforehand. A lot of the pain and loss is felt when the parent they have known and loved becomes so altered.

When a single person has lived with a parent for most of their lives and cared for them devotedly, the effect of the bereavement is likely to be felt in many different ways. For years, perhaps, their life has revolved round the needs of the elderly or sick parent, and care has been constant, night and day. Disturbed sleep has become a habit that will not be broken at once. If they have been used to rushing home from work or watching the clock during any stolen time with friends, they may find it hard to adapt to the fact that there is no longer any need to hurry back. Sometimes changing to a normal lifestyle may make them feel guilty. Guilt is a common ingredient of loss, and the 'if only' syndrome is familiar to those who counsel the bereaved. It is only too easy to remember those occasions when resentful words or cold behaviour spoilt the relationship. Now, the bereaved person may feel, 'Why didn't I hold my tongue? How could I have been so heartless?'

A couple who had looked after an elderly father in their home for many years, were persuaded at last to take one week's holiday. While they were away, he died. It was natural, but unreasonable, to feel guilt for what seemed like a failure in duty, rather than feel thankful for the years of unremitting and unselfish care that they had been able to give. It is important to try not to let the negative memories predominate but to remember instead the many good and happy times together. One friend in her mid-forties, who had cared for her demanding mother for a number of years, said, after her death, 'I don't feel any regrets at all. I did everything I could while Mother was alive. Now I'm free to make my own choices and to live my own life.'

Where social life has been jettisoned altogether in order to give adequate care, life without the dependent parent may seem empty and lonely. People vary in their ability to revert to being outgoing, social creatures after a long time of semi-confinement to the house. The kind of limitations imposed by restrictions of full-time caring are not normal to someone in midlife but it takes courage to change the pattern once the need to be restricted has passed. Even if it is not easy to make changes, it is important to begin widening horizons as soon as possible. Those who go to a church may find comfort and understanding there, as well as opportunities for wider social contact, in a sympathetic context.

The end of a chapter

When parents die, it seems as if part of your life has gone too. As one person put it, 'The only ones who knew me from the time I was born have gone, and it's almost as if that period in my life is less real now that there is no one left alive who shared it with me.' When both parents are dead there is no one to talk with about those uncertain, early memories of people and places, or to confirm when it was we had measles, or where we stayed on holiday. This absence of certainty seems to threaten our own identity. I still sometimes think — 'I'll ask

Mum about that,' only to realize that she is dead and no one remains who could possibly know or take interest in such small family details. Because I am a Christian, I have found the break less frightening, since I believe that my parents are now in the presence of the same God who is with me. The gulf between this life and the next is bridged by God's oneness and by his love and care over the living and the dead.

Unsafe

Death, particularly of someone close, brings a sense of insecurity. Although we know intellectually that the status quo cannot be maintained for ever, we feel profoundly disturbed when irreversible change actually happens. Nothing seems safe. Sometimes a person may experience several deaths in the family close together. One woman told me of a particular year in which seven close relatives died. I remember two aunts and an uncle, all very dear to me, dying within a few months. This kind of experience can reinforce our sense of insecurity, as well as making the burden of sadness unbearably heavy. At some stage it will be possible again to enjoy memories and to laugh at the fun we shared. But that is still in the future.

The older generation?

All the time that our parents are alive, we are the younger generation, at least to them. Once our parents are dead, we are catapulted into becoming the older generation ourselves. Most of us don't like it. We do not want to carry the image of middle age in other people's eyes, nor do we wish to think of ourselves as getting old. A glimpse in the mirror, or the well-meant comments of an old family friend, may remind us that we are growing to look like our parents. We may recognize their mannerisms in ourselves or find that we are talking to our children in just the tones that they talked to us. We have not only taken on the status of the older generation, we are beginning to look and behave that way too.

Above all, experiencing our parents' death forces us to face the fact of our own mortality. The inevitability of death becomes real for the first time. A universal truth has to be digested and made part of our thinking and understanding. For a while, thoughts of death can seem to dominate the whole of our everyday lives. In every newspaper at which we glance, the obituaries stare out at us. In every television news programme we hear of death, and in every letter or phone call from friends, someone's death is mentioned. Whether or not we have firmly held beliefs about what happens after death, we can still be terribly afraid. If our beliefs have never been challenged or put to the test we may doubt their validity now. All this may sound negative but it is more important to prepare for death than for any other event of life however much current thinking may sweep the subject under the carpet. If the death of our parents helps us to think about death in a constructive way and to prepare for our own, the experience is neither negative nor morbid but of positive value and importance.

If we have not done so before, now is the time to examine religious views and the firm hope of eternal life which is an integral part of the Christian faith and teaching. When Jesus was warning his followers about his own forthcoming death he told them not to be worried or upset but to put all their trust and confidence in him and in God. He told them that he was going to prepare a permanent home for them in God, the Father's, house. The apostle Paul, answering the anxious questions of Christians whose loved ones had died, reminded them that Jesus' own victory over death makes it certain that those who have come into a close relationship with him will share his new, full life which goes beyond the grave.

What shall we tell the children?
Small children who see grandparents frequently are likely to be distressed and puzzled by their death. The immediate problem for parents is what to tell them. Some fudge the issue by saying that the grandparent has gone away for a little while. Such a lie is unkind because it keeps false hope alive, as well as preventing the child from coming to terms with the parting and the inevitable grief. This kind of cop-out is also likely to undermine the parents' credibility and the trust put in them. It is always important to tell children the truth, in a way and at a level that they can accept. Many parents back off from telling children about death because they have no clear belief about it themselves. If that is so, they must explain something about that uncertainty to the child, and include the fact that others have a positive belief in life after death.

In Victorian times children were always taken to funerals but nowadays most people would not feel it was appropriate. A lot depends on what kind of occasion it is. I was recently at the funeral of a friend, who had died after a prolonged illness from cancer. Her six or seven grandchildren — none older than about nine or ten — were all there with their parents. Towards the end of the service, which had been full of praise and thanksgiving to God, the minister talked to them particularly. He told them a story about his own children, when they were very young.

'If we had been away and had a long night-time car journey ahead of us,' he said, 'we used to put the children in their pyjamas and wrap them in blankets before we started. They would soon go to sleep in the back of the car. When at last we got home, I would gently carry them indoors and put them into their beds, still asleep. Next morning they would wake up and find that they were at home. That is what has happened to your grandma. She was very tired, so while she was asleep, God, our Father, who she knew and loved dearly, took her to heaven. When she woke up, she found she was at home with him at last.'

Teenagers and older children also need to talk over their feelings about a grandparent's death, and perhaps examine beliefs about life after death. Whether they talk to you or to someone else may depend on the kind of relationship you have with them, as well as the stage which they are at. Many teenage children feel unable to talk to parents about intimate or emotional issues but it is important to be ready to talk, if they show that they want to.

The family estate

When the second parent dies, the family has to share out any money and possessions. This matter is made ten times easier if there is a will. It is important to encourage a remaining parent to make a new will. Even when there is a will, it will be six months or more before the beneficiaries have what is due to them.

As well as any money to be shared out, there are the bits and pieces, often not valuable in themselves, but relics of the family home which are closely associated with everyone's memories of early years. It is sad when sisters and brothers who have been on good terms quarrel about who gets what, whether the reasons for wanting a particular item are commercial or sentimental.

'Mother always wanted me to have. . . ' is not good enough. Legal advisers suggest that anyone wishing a piece of jewellery or other valuable to go to a particular person, should list such unofficial bequests on a piece of paper and keep it with the official will. When the family is all together, it is wise to suggest a fair method whereby family members (in-laws stand aside!) take turns to choose items great and small.

It is important not to risk giving cause for life-long resentments and recriminations. It is surprising how long this kind of grudge can be remembered, perhaps because the occasion is inextricably mixed with feelings of loss and deprivation caused by the parent's death. It is very important to keep on happy and good terms with the family that are living and it is extremely sad when the death of a parent who loved all the children should be an unwitting source of family rifts.

ACTION CHECKPOINTS

☐ Encourage parents to make a will, or a new one when necessary.

☐ Recognize that grief takes many forms.

☐ Take time to adjust to parents' death.

☐ Be honest in what you tell children about a grandparent's death.

☐ Begin to accept the responsibilities — and privileges — of being the 'older generation'.

☐ Don't duck the issues that death raises.

SECTION 4
THE YOUNGER GENERATION

9
COPING WITH TEENAGERS

The Things People Say

'I feel guilty, but I dislike my children intensely at times.'
Mother of teenagers

'I dread mine reaching their teens. Other mothers are always saying,
"I wish mine were still the age yours are."'
Mother of small children

'Everyone says how awful the teenage years are, and we had our share
of rows and problems, but I enjoyed those years with my children — far
better than the baby or toddler stages.'
Older mother

'A stormy passage through the Pulling Up Roots years will probably
facilitate the normal progression of the adult life cycle.'
Gail Sheehy, *Passages*

'How shall we pray for our children? . . . To pray is to collaborate with
God. It is to share his concern for our children.'
Dr John White, *Parents in Pain*

'Disciplining teenagers calls for discussion, reason, explanation and an
agreed way of dealing with the troubled situation for the benefit of all.'
Bringing Up a Family

'There is no ritual that provides children with a clear sign that
they have left infancy behind. . . So, unfortunately, parents and
children (or young adults) may disagree about what stage has been
reached and, consequently, what rights, privileges and responsibilities
are now appropriate.'
Martin Herbert, Professor of Psychology, *Living with Teenagers*

At midlife many people are not only facing the death of parents but also coping with difficult teenagers.

'Did you ever really dislike your children?' a mother of two teenage daughters asked me recently. She went on to admit, 'I feel guilty, but I dislike them intensely at times. I dread the mornings — wondering how they will come down — either sweet and reasonable or downright objectionable.'

A good many parents know exactly how she felt and could echo the same sentiments. But the adolescent years are not wholly fraught with stormy scenes, misery and rebellion. Many parents find themselves pleasantly surprised when the difficult stage passes with the minimum number of crises and heartbreaks.

The worst part of having children nearing their teens may be the fear of what is in store. Other parents do their best to frighten the life out of those who have not arrived at this stage, with doom-laden tales of trouble and strife. 'It gets much worse as they get older,' they warn darkly. As well as being a tactless comment, it is an exaggerated and often untrue one. I found the early years far harder to cope with than the teens and others often agree with me.

Certainly, parents who have had easy babies and amenable children may be unprepared for the changed behaviour that can characterize adolescence. There are also some people who 'specialize' in babies and young children and they may find it less easy to empathize with teenagers and handle them wisely. But many parents will welcome the arrival of the time when it is possible to share interests and to talk together in a more adult way. There are so many compensations for everyone in the family during the teenage years that it is a grave mistake to look on the black side. To fear the worst may be to have those fears come true.

No rites of passage?

In most tribal societies the transition from childhood to adulthood is clearly defined by 'rites of passage'. Initiation ceremonies of one kind or another mark the end of childhood and the acceptance of the boy or girl as an adult into the tribe. In our own society there is no such clear transition from childhood to adult life. The onset of puberty may occur as early as eleven or twelve and cannot be reckoned as the sign of having reached adult status. A young person officially comes of age at eighteen but, when so many go on to higher education and training after leaving school, even that does not mark the end of dependence on parents or state. To add to the uncertainty, the age at which a person is considered old enough to vote may be different from that at which they are allowed to marry or fight for their country.

If society is so confused about the age at which a person becomes an adult, it is not surprising if there are differences of opinion within the family too. Many of the rows and heartaches in the home crop up because adolescents think they are grown-up but the parents don't agree. Young people are keen to be granted the privileges of being adult, while parents major on the responsibilities involved. Sooner or later parents must let go, but the key issue is how much and how soon. Handling the whole process of letting go in a wise and loving way is probably the most important factor in negotiating the teenage years.

Change and change about

In our society, children often reach adolescence at just the time that their mothers are going through the menopause. The general sense of not being quite yourself, as well as the mood fluctuations and depression which often occur through hormonal imbalance are therefore going to hit both generations at the same time. In theory, this should make for greater understanding between the two, but teenagers are usually deeply absorbed in their *own* body and mood changes and have every excuse for not realizing that their mothers are suffering similarly and need some consideration too.

Both parents may also be coping with the doubts and identity crises which are common to midlife as well as to adolescence. Some parents have unhappy or embarrassing memories of their own teenage years. They may have tried to forget that period in their lives without coming to terms with some of the pain and guilt related to it. Seeing their own children in their teens may bring their own adolescence forcibly to mind, along with its unfinished business. Unless they come to terms with their own past adolescence, they will be unready to deal in a mature way with their children's.

Rivals?

Fathers and mothers may feel challenged by the looks, physical strength and sexual attractiveness of their sons and daughters. They do not want to be reminded of their own ageing by the evident blooming of youth at such close quarters. Parents who grew up in the sixties, when the cult of the teenager first took hold, may still look and feel young and be unready to acknowledge that their children are growing up. Many feel reluctant to take a back seat and allow their children to enjoy the special attractiveness of the teens and twenties.

Previous generations may also have felt a passing pang of regret as they allowed the younger generation to take their place, but they were not subjected to the pressure to stay young which affects men and women of forty or fifty today. On the credit side, there is probably a smaller gap between the two generations in outlook and interests. Provided that parents are able to come to terms with the possible jealousy and envy of their children, there is more scope for the two generations to enjoy easy friendship and to accept one another.

Understanding teenagers

Adolescence is the process of growing up. It is the period during which a boy or girl also grows from a child to an adult in body, mind and personality — a considerable transformation. The process usually coincides with the teen years but timing varies from one person to another. Growing out of childhood involves a great many major changes, so it is not surprising if teenagers seem totally self-absorbed and may sit for hours apparently doing nothing but day-dreaming. The adult who will finally emerge is different from the child, but still recognizably the same person you once knew and understood.

Puberty

Puberty marks the biological beginning of adult life. Until puberty, both boys and girls produce roughly similar quantities of both sex hormones, but at puberty there is a sharp increase in the secretion of sex-related hormones. It is these hormones which are responsible for the physical changes which occur. Girls are approximately two years ahead of boys in their development but there is a wide range in what is a normal age for a girl to reach puberty. Twelve is the present average age for the menarche — or start of menstrual periods, which marks puberty. But any time between eleven and fourteen is 'normal', although some girls may start as early as nine or ten or as late as fifteen or sixteen. Other physical changes which take place in the girl's body include development of the breasts, which may begin between eight and thirteen, and of the rounded feminine shape, as well as the growth of pubic hair.

Boys develop within a a similar age range of about five years, but most have reached puberty by the time they are sixteen. The clearest sign of puberty is ejaculation or emission, and glandular secretions also account for growth of the penis, growth of hair on the face and body, and the deepening of the voice.

The growth spurt in boys and girls often begins with the hands and feet, which is why they sometimes look a bit clumsy and act rather awkwardly, until the rest of the body catches up.

Reassurance

Both boys and girls need plenty of reassurance during this time of change and growth. They are often secretly tormented by fears that they are not normal, especially if they are early or late developers. A girl who is very tall for her age may fear that she will go on growing at the same rate indefinitely, while a boy who is shorter than his mates of the same age may be afraid that he will be permanently undersized. Time usually sorts out the discrepancies, but an explanatory book for them to read, or a reassuring chat, if you can talk things over with them, may save them a great deal of unnecessary anxiety. Some adolescents may need reassuring that there is nothing to be afraid of or ashamed about in night emissions or monthly periods.

Many teenagers worry, too, about whether they are attractive. They feel unsure about the way their bodies have changed and they need lots of encouraging comments and none of the wrong kind of remarks. Teasing a son or daughter about size or appearance is especially unkind at this stage. They are likely to get plenty of ribbing at school and need to feel accepted and approved at home.

Spots, and in some cases acne, can result from testosterone excess and it may help them to know that it is a passing affliction. Positive suggestions about diet and a cleansing routine may improve the condition and boost morale while the spots last. It is not surprising if boys and girls at this age spend hours in the bathroom, or in front of the mirror, adjusting to their new self. Help them to like what they see and to accept it with as much encouragement as you can give. If you feel worried yourself that growth or development may not be normal, consult the doctor to set your mind at rest.

Who am I?

The change from being a child to an adult involves a great deal more than physical and biological change. Some psychiatrists define mature adults as those who:

- think for themselves
- have their own goals
- have their own ideals
- can make and keep relationships
- can accept reality
- have respect for others' views and feelings.

In the light of such a definition some of us would admit that we still have some growing up to do ourselves. So it is not surprising that adolescents sometimes make heavy weather of the whole process. As they try to find out who they are they may experiment with a number of different modes. They may adopt clothes and hairstyles that belong to one group of contemporaries or another, and change their political or religious views several times. Some make their parents anxious by the kind of friends they choose and the models they copy.

In order to find their own identity and to become persons in their own right, many young people feel it necessary to rebel against the attitudes and beliefs of their parents. They may reject what they regard as middle-class or old-fashioned values and delight in looking as dirty and scruffy as possible, championing people and causes that most of the people their parents mix with would not consider acceptable. Those with a particular political or religious upbringing may react strongly against that. In these ways, they force their parents to recognize that they are no longer a mere extension of them or the family, but independent human beings with views and ambitions of their own. The ways in which teenagers make their point may differ, but that is the message they are trying to get across.

Boys in particular need to cut the umbilical cord. Instinctively they fear the strength of the emotional ties with their mother, which could prevent them from becoming mature and independent men. The way in which they try to break those ties may often be brutal and very painful for the mother, but the instinct is right. The more she can stop herself 'mothering' her son in the old familiar way, the sooner he will feel that it is 'safe' to be close to her, without risk to his own manhood. The new relationship which can then develop between mother and son can be rich and rewarding for them both.

Minor scuffles may also break out between father and sons. Teenage boys, like young bulls in a herd, often jockey for position and want to try out their own strength. A wise father will recognize the reason for his sons' aggressive or needling behaviour and remain firm but cool himself without feeling threatened or provoked.

Letting go

All wise parents eventually recognize the need to let go. The burning question is — how soon? Disagreement about the rate at which parents let go is usually the root of the trouble. For example, a girl of fourteen may reckon that she is old enough to go camping abroad or inter-state with an assorted group of friends of her own age. When parents refuse, there is either an almighty bust-up or a continuing groundswell of discontent that lasts for weeks. If you are unlucky, you may get both.

While the girl sees the trip as a reasonable privilege for a fourteen-year-old, you recognize that she and a group of young teenagers are not ready to handle the responsibilities and possible risks involved. Both parties are looking at the project from different angles, so it is not surprising if each fails to see the other's viewpoint.

If parents keep cool and explain fully why they are saying no, they make it easier for their daughter to back down without losing face. They may also be able to build in some safeguards which would make it possible for them to give permission. For example, there might be one or two parents, or some older, responsible young people, who could accompany the younger ones.

Learning to be responsible

Teenagers have to learn that privilege and responsibility go hand in hand. Sometimes, as in the case of a foreign or inter-state trip, the youngster may just not be old enough or experienced enough to cope, but at other times they may not be showing enough sense of responsibility to be safely granted privileges. Teenagers who consistently fail to let parents know when they will be home, or where they are likely to be, cannot expect to be allowed to stay out to all hours. Once young people recognize the perfectly reasonable link between being responsible and having privileges granted, they may be more inclined to co-operate. Parents who themselves behave in a responsible way towards their children, making it a habit to keep them informed of their whereabouts and accounting for their own actions, are more likely to receive the same consideration in return.

Human beings do not usually shoulder responsibility by choice. They have to be taught and encouraged to do so. Some parents fail to give their teenagers the opportunity or incentive to be responsible, yet complain that they still behave like children. If a teenager decides to earn money doing a paper round, or a Saturday job, there is no reason why their mother should set her alarm in order to wake them at an unearthly hour. Getting up and being at the shop on time is the teenager's own responsibility and part of the cost to be reckoned with.

What kind of parent?

Psychologists describe parental attitudes to teenagers as ranging from:

- warm and loving, to hostile and rejecting

- restrictive and controlling, to permissive
(encouraging autonomy)

These two sets of attitudes may be combined in various ways. A loving parent may also be controlling, that is, unwilling to allow the teenager to make decisions or be responsible in any way. Similarly, a rejecting parent may allow the child to behave as he or she likes. It is also possible to combine a rejecting and an authoritarian attitude, or a loving and a permissive one.

All parents fit in somewhere along the scale, differing from one another in their handling of the young adults in the family. There is no one right way to behave, but it is clear that teenagers suffer when parents overprotect, as well as when they leave them to their own devices and appear not to care.

When parents are so concerned for the children's safety that they prevent them from exercising choice and making decisions, they are depriving them of the experience they need in order to cope with life as mature adults. On the other hand, parents who show no sign of caring where their youngsters are, or what they are doing, not only leave them free to get into all kinds of trouble but make it harder for them to take responsibility by depriving them too soon of parental care. Your teenager may insist that no one else's parents are as strict as you are, but adolescents need the security that reasonable and clearly defined parental limits provide.

A group of young teenage girls once admitted to me that although they frequently complained because their parents insisted that they should be home by a certain time, they recognized that the deadline gave them a useful excuse for not getting out of their depth. It also reassured them that their parents loved them and cared about their well-being.

Loving without conditions

It is very important that teenagers should never feel rejected by their parents, either because the parents really have given up on them or else because they treat them with coldness and apparent disapproval or dislike. Whatever youngsters do, rejection can never be the right reaction. Even when parents strongly disapprove of the way their teenager is behaving, it is still important to make it clear that it is the behaviour and not the person that is being rejected.

On paper this may sound like splitting hairs, but in practice it is perfectly possible to make the difference clear. Unless parents are on their guard, they may often give the impression that they have withdrawn love and acceptance, just at the time when both are most needed. Love must be seen to survive the worst rows and the most unlikeable or painful behaviour. At a time when no one else may seem to approve of them, and they may not much like themselves, it is of the utmost importance that teenagers should feel wanted and loved by their parents.

Staying friends

Parents as well as their children need to be aware that the relationship between them is changing and developing into one that is more equal and reciprocal. The old pattern of family life, where everyone existed and acted under the family umbrella, is fast disappearing. It is possible for parents to go on behaving as they have always done towards their children, without making adjustments as they are needed. They may put the blame entirely on the teenagers for failing to respond to their advice or orders as they once did, but the fault may be theirs for failing to treat them as the young adults they have now become.

Parents who enjoy a happy relationship with their own parents, may find it easier to adapt to a new kind of relationship with their own fast-maturing children. Eventually, the children of the family will take their place as adults whose views and opinions carry as much weight as those of their parents. The relationship should still be special and unique, but it will only survive as something good and precious if it is allowed to grow into a friendship between equals.

Keep talking

Some break in communications between parents and children often occurs during teenage years. Usually no permanent damage is done and the confrontations of the stormy years are forgiven and forgotten. But there is the sad possibility that parent and child stop communicating at this time and never rebuild the relationship on a new and satisfying footing. There will probably be rows and outbursts on the part of both teenagers and parents, but if these are kept from degenerating into resentments, dislike and misunderstanding at a deep and continuing level, there will be little harm done. Parents and children both desperately need each other's love and respect and it is important to let it be seen that you still accept and value one another, even in the midst of the turbulent years of the teens. It is the parents who must set an example of consideration and true courtesy to the teenagers, whether they seem to deserve it or not.

Parents and children need to keep talking to each other. It may seem at times that there is little common ground between the two generations, but if a parent is patient and ready to take an interest, and to listen as well as to give advice or pass criticism, there is plenty to talk about and share together. When the children were six months or six years old, it was a fairly straightforward matter recognizing their needs and being available at times that could also be fitted neatly into your own routine. Now there is no knowing when you may be needed and not everyone finds it easy to be on hand to talk or listen when required.

It is important not only to give time but to be genuinely interested in your teenagers and in what interests them. Caustic remarks about their latest pop or sports idol don't help. Many teenagers are willing to listen, too, to what interests or worries you. Quality matters more than quantity in the time you spend together. It is worth sounding a warning to those who are part of a tightly-knit family unit. Teenagers do not want parents *too* interested or involved in their world. A teenager whose parent is her 'best friend' may be failing to find the friends that she should have among her peers and those outside the family group. Parents should not try to monopolize their teenagers, with however good a motive. It can hinder their proper development.

If you and your children have always talked together on all kinds of subjects, you may find it easier to sit down and talk reasonably and quietly about some of the hard decisions that have to be made. Whether the issue is whether to buy a motor

motor bike, what college or university to apply for, or what job to look for, a calm discussion of all the factors involved is far more fruitful than teenage demand met by flat parental refusal, with no real thinking on either side. Parents need to listen as well as to talk and to let it be seen that they recognize the teenager's viewpoint, even when they take an opposite view. On the other hand, they also need to explain their own good reasons for a decision, and refuse to give in to teenage threats or tears, when they know that decision is right. Every time a problem is solved by reasonable and rational discussion, the way is made easier for similar problem-solving in the future.

Right and wrong

Many parents who have given their children a clear understanding of right and wrong, and those who have laid the foundation of Christian faith, may feel at this stage that their children are rejecting their values once and for all. Sometimes such a thing does happen. It may happen when parents have indoctrinated their children, that is, laid down a set of beliefs without allowing the children freedom to think for themselves and to come up with their own reactions. It is very important to give children room to think for themselves and not to impose on them a restricting interpretation of truth. It is also important to practise what you preach. Faith is better caught than taught and the example of a parent is a strong influence even while teenagers seem to be rejecting what you taught them.

A boy or girl who appears to be rejecting parental values may be developing in a more healthy and normal way than one who follows the parent's party line and gives no trouble. Young people must discover faith for themselves and make it truly their own if they are to find a foundation for life. Second-hand beliefs are not much help in the real world and adolescents who merely assent to what they are taught will find those beliefs of very little use when serious problems of life arise. Parents need patience.

When to say no

Parents sometimes need to exercise their authority and say no. It is important to keep reviewing the matter of what to allow and what to refuse. It is also important to judge each case on its merits. It is also important to decide whether the particular issue warrants bringing out all the big guns. Rules and prohibitions are best accepted and obeyed when they are kept to a minimum and when good reasons are put forward for abiding by them. All good parents forbid what is dangerous to their child, whether the danger is physical or moral. It may still be important to say no, on those grounds, even to older teenagers. Parents may see danger when their children are too inexperienced to recognize it. The teenager's own responsibleness — and that of their friends — will have a bearing on your decision.

Does the son who wants a motor bike show signs of being ready to handle a potentially lethal machine? Does he respect the safety measures laid down? Does the daughter who wants to go to a party where there will be unlimited alcohol have the confidence, sense and moral courage to take a different line, if necessary, from her friends? No hard and fast rules can be laid down, but the sooner you can help teenagers acquire the confidence to act responsibly and not to be afraid of peer pressure, the more freedom you can allow them. You are also preparing them well for the time when they will be outside your jurisdiction for ever.

Keeping the contract

Martin Herbert, a professor of clinical psychology, has written an excellent book, *Living with Teenagers*. He outlines a plan for coping with the conflicts that often arise in the family during the teenage years. He suggests that parents and child should draw up a contract between them, with both making promises which cannot be altered without joint agreement. Usually, he suggests, it is better to put the agreement into writing, with a relative or family friend as witness.

The kind of promises each party to the contract makes will vary, but one fairly typical example is for the teenager to promise to tidy his bedroom once a week, to let parents know when he will be late home from school or where he is and who he is with when he goes out. In return, parents might promise not to keep criticizing his friends, to give an increased allowance of pocket money and to be ready to admit when they are in the wrong. As well as penalties laid down for breaking the contract (perhaps no evenings out for a given period?), there need to be rewards for keeping it, perhaps in the form of a family treat.

Professor Herbert argues that such an arrangement is neither cold-blooded nor out of keeping for a family. After all, most relationships are based on contracts, whether written, spoken or just taken for granted. Friendship as well as marriage is a two-way affair and it is only when both parties have the opportunity to share problems, experiences and ideas and to give as well as take, that the relationship is a success. During the teen years it is only too easy to misinterpret the role of both parent and child with a lot of consequent hot air and bad feeling. Sitting down together to work out what are reasonable contributions to the relationship on both sides satisfies the teenager's sense of fairness and cuts out the constant nagging, pleading and resentment that so quickly sours the good relationship that parents and children need to enjoy together.

ACTION CHECKPOINTS

☐ Prepare to enjoy the teen years.

☐ Take time to talk to your teenagers.

☐ Never stop loving and accepting your teenagers.

☐ Adapt to their new needs — recognize that they are growing up.

☐ Think before saying yes — or no.

☐ Consider the value of a family contract.

☐ Prepare to play the waiting game.

10
SPECIAL CASES

The Things People Say

'Only roughly half adopted children wish to discover their birth parents. They feel perfectly at home with their adoptive family, yet they are conscious that they also belong elsewhere.'
Senior social worker with adopted teenagers

'Natural parents also have children at this stage who don't fit in.'
Social worker

'Remember clashes are common in all families. They just tend to be more intense in stepfamilies.'
Erica De'Ath, *Teenagers Growing up in a Stepfamily*

'Whether we like it or not, the stepfamily is the family of the future and society has a duty to accept this.'
Elizabeth Hodder, in *The Times*

'The day when I attached less importance to (my stepdaughter) liking me than to her respecting me, I began to treat her more as I would my own child.'
Elizabeth Hodder, *The Step-parents Handbook*

'Trying to make changes right away only results in rejected efforts, and sometimes creates other problems. Children are influenced most by example and by the kind of person the step-parent is.'
Einstein and Albert

'Many parents bring me rebellious teenagers with the plea, "Please change her, doctor!" But I can't change anyone who doesn't want to be changed.'
Dr John White, *Parents in Pain*

Some parents recognize that their family or their particular teenagers are different in some way or another. Often, the usual guidelines still apply, but it may be reassuring to highlight and comment on a few of the special situations in which some parents are placed.

Parents whose children have a handicap or disablement represent one such large group. Adolescence will be a time for facing new situations and some burning issues about the need for independence, employment and 'dating'. The needs are so varied and require such specialist and informed help that it is not possible to deal with them here. Many support groups have sprung up in recent years, at national and local level, to support and advise families of those suffering from specific diseases or forms of disablement. Other group members in similar circumstances can understand and offer help from their own experience.

The adopted family

Couples who wish to adopt a child are likely to find that conditions of acceptance are strict, and preliminary preparation and training sessions prolonged and stringent. This is especially the case when the boy or girl to be adopted has a disability or a disturbed background. Parents who succeed in adopting a child are likely to take the whole matter of their upbringing even more seriously and conscientiously than many who have given birth to their children.

At adolescence, adopted children have the normal crop of teenage problems. Parents may jump to the conclusion that the fact of being adopted is the root of the trouble when that has nothing to do with the case. A senior social worker with an adoption society, who deals specifically with the needs of teenagers, confirms this fact. She emphasizes the importance of parents coming to terms with the full implications of adoption from the very beginning. Provided that they have done so, and that the child has been matched with them as carefully as possible so that they can best meet his or her needs, their situation is likely to be no different from that of any other family with teenagers. Natural parents find it just as hard to understand and meet the needs of their adolescent children. Unfortunately, a doctor or psychologist may sometimes reinforce parents' concern by remarking, 'Well, of course, he's adopted,' when this has nothing to do with the matter in question. The problems are the normal ones of adolescence and will pass in their own good time.

Who am I?

Adolescents, like their midlife parents, are searching for their identity. For adopted children that quest may include tracing their natural or birth parents. Roughly half the children who are adopted feel an urgent need to discover their origins. Since 1976, in Britain at least, anyone of eighteen or over has been allowed by law to go to the General Register Office, the local Social Services or the appropriate adoption agency to obtain their original birth certificate. They are also required to see a counsellor. After that they are free to carry out the search for their birth parents.

Some teenagers are deterred through fear of hurting the feelings of their adopted parents and others may have too many doubts as to how the encounter might work out. Some make preliminary enquiries then wait a few years but many feel it is so desperately important to know where they came from and who they belonged to that they go ahead. Their search in no way means that they are dissatisfied with their adopted home or love their adopted parents any the less. But they feel that they belong to two families and, as one girl put it, 'I was part of that woman's body for nine months', so discovering her birth-mother's identity seemed, to her, an urgent necessity.

It is easy for adopted parents to feel hurt or rejected and it is only rarely that they and the child make the search together. It may be hard for them to go on giving warmth and understanding love amidst the euphoria and excitement that can surround the search for the birth parents and their possible discovery. But the teenager is likely to need the reassurance and loving security of the familiar home and parents more than ever during this traumatic time.

Midlife search

It is worth mentioning at this point that many people who were adopted as babies feel the need in midlife to search out their natural parents. They were not legally entitled to do so as teenagers and various factors may trigger their desire to find their birth parents at this stage. It may be that the death of their adopted parents leaves them free to make inquiries without giving them hurt. It also reminds them that their natural parents must be growing old too, and that the time for finding them is limited. They may have come upon documents relating to their early life when they cleared out the dead parents' papers. Any of these factors, as well as the renewed need to know and understand themselves which occurs at midlife, may lead to a belated search for their roots.

The reconstituted family

By the end of the century about half of all children in Britain will have acquired at least one stepfather — however temporarily — by the time they are sixteen. Two out of five families are already full-time or part-time stepfamilies. The reconstituted, or stepfamily, is formed when two partners marry, one or both bringing children from a previous relationship with them. The new marriage may follow death, separation or (most usually) divorce of the previous partner. Sometimes the new couple themselves are so much in love that they have unreasonably high expectations for the whole new family that will be formed. But not all the people involved have made a conscious choice to create this unit.

The ending of one relationship and the beginning of another is a complex matter. It will take time, self-awareness and unselfish giving on the part of the couple themselves, and of all the other parties concerned, if the new relationships are to succeed. More second marriages break down because of the children of the partners than for any other single cause. When teenage children are involved, as full-time or part-time members of the new family, there is considerable added pressure. It is very important that their specific needs and difficulties are taken into account. Remember:

● They may still be mourning the loss of the parent who has died or left home.

● They long above everything for their two parents to be reunited. They may still have fantasies of such a reunion after one or both have remarried.

● Their loyalties may be divided — they have a longer previous family history with both parents than young children and may feel torn between loyalty and love for both.

● They may have had the unsettling experience of living in three different households — the original family, an interim family with only one parent — and the newly-formed stepfamily.

● They have not chosen the new family and they may not feel love or even liking for the new partner.

● They may fear to extend love and acceptance to the new partner as it seems a betrayal of the absent parent.

● They may wonder where they belong. Many are uprooted, having to leave home, school and friends. Part-time step-children may have no room to themselves in their weekend or holiday family.

● They may dislike or be jealous of new step-brothers or sisters.

● Their status in the new family may be radically changed. A previous eldest may now be youngest, or the other way round.

● Sexual jealousy may play a part in their reactions, especially where a new partner is brought into the home before marriage.

Parent wisdom
The role of step-parents can be hard, especially if the problems have not been foreseen and the marriage has taken place on a powerful wave of emotion and little else. The head-shakings and prognostications of family and friends may have been ignored completely. It is vital to face up to some of the problems inherent in the situation and to be as honest as possible about all the relationships involved. Many step-parents feel guilty for not loving their step-children in the way they do their own. A younger person marrying and taking on a teenage family may know very little about adolescents. She would do well to learn more, from books or from other parents, about the stage through which the step-children are passing.

It is very important that the two partners endeavour to:

● Agree on discipline. Perhaps the step-parent needs to work out his or her own approach to disciplining the teenager.

● Talk together about any problems as honestly as possible.

● Refuse to sweep difficulties under the carpet but sort things out even when it is painful.

● Avoid money discussions in front of the teenagers. Money is the second highest cause for breakdown of second marriages. Teenagers are said to be especially sensitive to the financial implications and aware of their own lack of power in the matter.

● Make ground rules for behaviour. This is especially important when teenagers come for weekends or holidays only. They may stay in bed to all hours, slump in front of the television and expect to be waited on hand, foot and finger. Firm but gentle provision and enforcement of basic rules is kinder to them and necessary for your survival.

● Stop resentments building up. Sort things out as you go — as every family needs to do.

Elizabeth Hodder, whose wisdom I have relied upon in this section, found from personal experience that there was no help available for stepfamilies in Britain. So she founded The National Stepfamily Association. She sums up the situation by saying that the reconstituted family is never the same as the biological family. It can be satisfying and good, but it is different. Her comment is: 'High expectations spell disaster — low expectations and there may be a chance of survival.' She recommends too that targets should be short-term ones. That way, even a small success gives a sense of achievement and provides something positive for the new family to build upon. All the qualities normally required for coping with adolescents are needed in the stepfamily — tolerance, reasonable guidelines and discipline, respect and good communication. Above all, patience is needed to work out new situations and relationships, in a family which has no shared past.

When things go wrong

Many people today believe that children begin life with a clean slate. Parents are largely responsible for providing the right environment so that their children grow up happy, balanced and free from hang-ups. Later on, school, peer groups and society influence the child's development too. The logical result of such thinking is that parents feel largely responsible when things go wrong. They often suffer deep feelings of guilt if their children fail to succeed, to make good relationships or to turn into responsible and law-abiding members of society. Psychiatrists and other advisers may reinforce this attitude.

The Christian belief about people, based on biblical teaching, is different. Human beings have good and loving feelings, because God is love and we were originally made in God's image. But something went badly wrong. Because people refused — and still do refuse — to live life as it was meant to be lived, in happy friendship and obedience to God, evil is present, not only in our world, but within us all. Crimes against society, such as theft, murder and outright war, as well as bad actions against family and friends, spring from our inborn desire to get our own way and do what we want, however much we normally keep those feelings under control.

The parent of a new-born child is not providing all the input for a mind blank of any social or moral bias, but is dealing with a personality that will display a bundle of mixed motives and behaviour. Wise and loving training will help the growing child to foster tendencies and characteristics which are beneficial to society and helpful to the child's development. But however good their upbringing, young people are still free to throw over the controls and act in a selfish and destructive way. Everyone, however conditioned by family and society, still retains the dignity and freedom given by God, of exercising their own will and choosing good or evil.

Dr John White, a psychiatrist, comments: 'There are general rules. Good parents are less likely to produce problem children than bad parents. Stable homes are more likely to produce stable children than unstable homes. But that's as far as it seems to go. There are no steel-reinforced rules which say: Good parenting always produces good children. Bad parenting always produces bad children. It simply isn't true.'

Positive encouragements

There are ways in which parents can encourage their growing children to make right choices in life. Children and teenagers have a head start if they have:

• a stable family unit

• parents who love and care for each other and for them

• clear teaching from early days about the difference between right and wrong

• gradual encouragement to develop self-control and to practise consideration for others

• the example of parents or others with a sincere and non-legalistic faith, which they live as well as teaching wisely

• increasing freedom to make choices within a framework of secure guidelines

• honesty and openness among family members and freedom to talk out problems

• shared time, interests and enjoyments with their parents

Anorexia nervosa

Adolescent girls are the commonest victims of anorexia nervosa. The real causes of the disease are still a mystery. Although sufferers appear to have lost their appetite — which is what the word anorexia literally means — their chief worry is weight increase. Anorexics have a false idea of their own appearance, seeing themselves as fat even when they have become painfully thin. Most anorexics have a low opinion of themselves and see losing weight as their most important goal in order that others will value them and so that they can respect themselves. Some anorexics combine fasting with occasional binges, followed by self-induced purging or vomiting. Monthly periods often stop altogether. It is very important for parents to get professional help as soon as they recognize any of these warning signs.

Smoking

It's an encouraging if surprising fact that children and young people are much less likely to smoke when parents tell them that they don't want them to. It is better still when parents set them the right example by not smoking themselves. Young people are unlikely to be affected by statistics showing the high incidence of disease and early death among smokers. But parents, who know those facts, can use all their influence to discourage the habit. The myths that link smoking with glamour, with being adult or having sex appeal need to be firmly exploded. Fortunately, some well-known figures in the sports and pop world are helping to do this. (See also chapter 4 on smoking.)

Alcohol

A recent medical report expressed concern about increased drinking among boys and girls, including those under the legal age. According to its findings almost half the accidental deaths among teenagers over fifteen in Britain is caused by alcohol. Forty-five per cent of fatal road accidents involving young people are alcohol-linked, and so are drowning and deaths from accidental overdose. Government money is needed to educate young people about the dangers of alcohol, but unless there is back-up in the family, such a campaign is unlikely to succeed. Many parents in midlife come to rely heavily on alcohol themselves, to help them cope with stresses and pressures at home or work. Teenagers may imitate their example. Young people are best able to withstand the danger of alcohol abuse if they have been taught:

- the danger to health of too much alcohol — and how much is too much

- how to say No without losing face with their peers

- that drinking too much is not clever or a sign of being grown-up

- that alcohol is not a problem-solver or a sexual stimulant — the opposite in both cases

- that too much alcohol can kill

- never to drink and drive

In all these cases, it is vitally important that parents should set an example. (See chapter 4.)

Drugs

Parents who worry about their teenage children getting involved with drugs, are normally thinking of drugs other than tobacco and alcohol. They are concerned about those drugs that are forbidden by law. Teenagers may begin to take drugs to help them escape from adolescent problems they can't cope with. Some of the illegal and dangerous drugs include the following:

Solvent abuse Sniffing glue — and other agents — is often more common among children and young teenagers. Since the substances used are often freely on sale for legitimate purposes, it is hard to crack down on this form of abuse. Many young people who carry on the habit on their own, after first experimenting with friends, are trying to escape from unhappiness at home, perhaps because their parents are quarrelling.

Cannabis Teenagers often insist that cannabis is harmless, but it has been shown to be a high risk for certain users. It is also illegal. There is some evidence that it can cause schizophrenia. Cannabis users sometimes go on to use dangerous hard drugs.

Heroin and cocaine These are the best known of the hard drugs. Cocaine smuggling has increased alarmingly. Most parents are aware of the very severe risk to life in using such drugs and of the increased danger, to those who inject and share needles, of contracting AIDS or hepatitis B.

The most obvious sign of drug-taking in a young person is a change in personality. A quiet teenager may become aggressive or a normally outgoing cheerful one become unnaturally withdrawn. They may be lethargic or irritable and lose interest in their usual hobbies, school work or sport. Of course, all these symptoms can be part of the growing-up process, but if you are worried that your teenager might be taking drugs, or suspect drug-taking among their friends or school mates, it is very important for their own safety that you should get help. They are also breaking the law and could be in serious trouble for that. In most countries there are clinics and advice centres with a free phone line. The doctor or a social worker could also advise.

Homosexuality

Attitudes to homosexuality and lesbianism in our society range from complete rejection to acceptance of it as a valid alternative to a heterosexual preference. It is extremely difficult to make any statement, however carefully worded, without being accused of extremism by one side or the other. Many Christians accept the fact that a proportion of people are homosexual through no fault or voluntary choice of their own. But that fact does not make homosexual *practice* part of God's plan for the human race, which is based on the loving, permanent relationship of one man and one woman. In this respect the 'condition' calls for the same personal discipline as a celibate single life. At the same time, others need to offer the caring, understanding support which helps to make such a life possible.

It is important for parents:

● to remember that teenagers normally go through the phase of being attracted to someone of the same sex. This is part of growing up and has nothing to do with a deep-seated homosexual tendency.

● to protect teenage children during this phase from contact with those who might exploit them and places where that might occur.

● to be able to talk with their teenagers openly and without undue emotion on the subject, explaining their own beliefs.

● to get skilled advice if they have reason to believe that their teenager may be genuinely homosexual.

● to give love, understanding and acceptance to their son or daughter, whatever their tendency.

Teenage pregnancy

The attitude to unmarried mothers is very different now from a generation ago, but it is still a tragedy for most families if a schoolgirl daughter becomes pregnant. The girl herself will probably be thoroughly frightened, however she may try to hide the fact. It is important that:

- parents and daughter should talk freely about the future

- parents should still show love and acceptance as well as giving support

- thorough counselling is asked for

- that the girl's own wishes are considered

- that decisions are made for the right reasons and do not run counter to deeply held attitudes or beliefs

- parents aim to use the crisis to strengthen bonds with their daughter.

Depression

During adolescence, emotions are strong and teenagers often experience violent mood swings, including bouts of depression. When depression is severe, it is an illness requiring medical attention. Signs of clinical depression include: a marked change in patterns of eating and sleeping, inability to concentrate, extreme lethargy and deep unhappiness (see chapter 5). Depression may sometimes lead to suicide threats or attempts. Although attempted suicide has increased among older teenagers, the rate is still well below that for adults. But such threats should never be treated lightly. They are often a cry for help. It is not true that those who threaten to kill themselves never do. Consult your doctor in order to be referred for specialist help.

Professional help

Parents who recognize that they are out of their depth should always seek help. They may talk first to someone wise and experienced — a person they know and can confide in. They may also need professional help and their family doctor, church minister, head teacher or social worker, could refer them to a psychologist, psychotherapist, psychiatrist or counsellor from a specialist organization.

Many parents experience deep pain and despair about their teenage children. Most will have discovered by this time that love involves risk. When we love we are vulnerable. We fear the pain and hurt that may touch those we love but we lay ourselves open to hurt and pain from them. Love also involves risk. Having a child means taking an enormous risk in emotional terms, as well as in other ways. We have been responsible for launching our children into life and are well aware that we have made the usual crop of mistakes, even though we have tried our hardest to do what is best for them. Most of what follows, now that they are nearly grown up, is not within our power to decide. We cannot be accountable for the choices that our children are going to make, even though we have contributed to those choices. We have to leave them to be independent and responsible people in their own right. But, not surprisingly, many parents continue to feel anxious, tense and sad about their children.

I have been through all these emotions myself. I found comfort — although at times I had to struggle to do so — from knowing that God is the Father, *par excellence*, and he therefore knew exactly how I was feeling. Better still, he loves my children even more than I do and wants what is best for them. I prayed for them in their growing up years more than I had ever done before. I prayed that God would protect them, now that I no longer could, and that he would bring them close to him too. I have also learned to pray that God will do what he sees is best for them.

Now, a number of years later, I have seen some of God's plans for them come about and realize how much he has cared for them and kept them safe. John White, who writes both as a psychiatrist and as a father, comments in *Parents in Pain*, 'I do not know what destiny whether small or great God plans for the children who most concern you. I do know that you will have more peace if you can grasp how crucial relinquishment is, how utterly safe it is to place your children in God's sure hands.'

ACTION CHECKPOINTS

☐ Keep the idea of 'special cases' in proportion — many teenagers have problems.

☐ Get help from specialist agencies when needed.

☐ Give teenagers positive instruction on dangers of: smoking, alcohol, other drugs.

☐ Get advice, if concerned, about: anorexia, drugs, depression.

☐ Consider if faith in God and prayer may help you — and your teenagers.

11
NEW SITUATIONS

The Things People Say

'The empty nest can lead to greater maturity. We are free to give time to those who are like ourselves, or like we were once, or like we shall be one day.'
Speaker at conference on Midlife

'Two out of the three are away at college — I haven't missed them much yet. I don't want them to feel guilty about leaving home.'

'One of our sons was with us for eight months before going away to the other end of the earth — I couldn't even phone him. I had a tremendous sense of bereavement — it hurt inside — I had no idea it would be like that.'
Mother of four children

'One daughter was married on the Saturday and our son went abroad on the Monday and our third child married eighteen months later. I was not going to be one of those mothers who cried, and I didn't.'

'The past exists in every stepfamily but a remarriage is a commitment to the future. . . Don't feel depressed if movement is slow. . . the most important thing is to give yourself, the parents and the children time.'
Booklet for step-grandparents by The National Stepfamily Association

'His grandchildren call me Auntie, and I love looking after them when they come. But when Brian goes to see them he goes with his first wife, who they call Granny. I ask you, how are the children going to understand that it's Brian and I who are married? How will they see me?'
Young step-grandmother

'Grandchildren are wonderful. They give so much joy and then you can always hand them back when you've had enough.'

'It's amazing to see how differently the grandchildren in the various families are brought up. One lot are as good as gold — we'll have them any day, but another lot are almost more than we can cope with! But we say nothing!'

Mothers belong to a small group of people whose success is measured by how well they work themselves out of their job. They recognize that their overall goal is to launch their child into the world, as an independent and responsible young adult. But they may find themselves unprepared for the pain and the sense of loss that the achieving of that goal may bring in its wake.

Writers about midlife are fond of referring to the empty nest syndrome, much to the annoyance of feminists, who deplore the notion that women need children to bolster their sense of self-worth. But however we label this stage, it is clear that many, if not most, women experience a quite severe sense of loss when their children leave home. Fathers may miss their teenagers but are not likely to grieve in the same way. When the marriage is good, a husband may be able to encourage his wife to see the many compensations in store, including the opportunities to explore their own interests and reinforce their commitment to each other.

It may seem ironic to onlookers that the very parents who have been complaining loud and long about the difficulty of sharing their home with impossible teenage children, should be lamenting the fact that they've left, only a few months later.

In some areas and in some social groups, children continue to live at home until they marry. The difficult period of adolescence passes and the relationship between parents and children becomes workable and often happy. But in many cases boys and girls leave home at around eighteen to get work, for further training, or to go to university. In fact, just as the difficult teens are coming to an end, the young adults are off.

It is natural that parents, and mothers in particular, should feel sadness and a sense of bereavement, whether or not they have been full-time housewives and mothers. One woman, who already had a job and a busy life of her own, was surprised to find how sad she felt when her children left home in quick succession.

'I thought it would be good to be free to get on with my own affairs,' she said, 'but I suffered quite severe depression. In many ways I've had a fuller and more satisfying life since then, and I know that my children still need me in lots of ways. But at the time I felt rejected and useless, because I wasn't needed in the way I had been for so long.'

Another mother, whose three children left home the same summer — the twins on the same day — described her sensation of being left in a vacuum.

'It was a feeling of being suspended — it was not a negative feeling and not even a loss to be mourned, but I just could not see a way ahead. That feeling of uncertainty did not last long, I found a new pathway and the bewilderment soon went. But I do now sometimes wish that I had given them more time when I did have them.'

Single parents are likely to find the experience even more traumatic. It may be the first time that they have had to live alone and that a whole new way of life has to be taken on board at a time when they are emotionally upset and feeling the sadness of being parted from their son or daughter.

A psychiatrist emphasized the importance of preparing for the emotion of loss and recognizing it when it comes. He described one woman who kept saying, 'I can't wait for my second one to leave home,' but was actually denying the sadness she felt. When genuine feelings are denied and pushed down, depression may follow.

Learning independence
On the credit side, there is much for the parents as well as the teenagers to gain when the time comes for them to leave home. The children learn to take responsibility for themselves. However hard parents try to inculcate a sense of responsibility in their children, the habits of childhood die hard. Most mothers haven't the heart to deny their children the care and comfort they have given them all their lives and many continue to run round them long after they are old enough to look after themselves. In order to become a responsible adult, a young man or woman must learn the cost of living, in terms of hard cash and hard work. While they are living at home, so many things are thrown in free. It can come as a shock to have to buy every stamp, tube of toothpaste or bar of soap as well as to wash and press favourite clothes before going out, and to change and launder their own bed linen.

Young people away from home for the first time also have to find the resources within themselves to create a pattern of living. Up to now, they have conformed, perhaps unwillingly, to the family's routine. One student described her feelings in her first weeks at university. She realized that if she chose she could go all day without food and go to bed at any hour she liked. No one was likely to know or care. She recognized that she had to make a sensible framework of her own.

For these reasons, and many more, no teenager returns home, even after a few months away, without having changed. The family may look forward to the first visit home, assuming that everything can go on exactly where it left off. The parents may not have changed but the teenager most certainly will have done. There is likely to be a far greater appreciation of home comforts but there may also be a reluctance to answer the barrage of questions or to say much about the new life. But, provided that parents are patient and do not ask too many questions too soon, they will usually hear something of what's going on. And with that they must be content.

Setting them free
Adults have the right to make decisions for themselves. Wise parents give their children increasing freedom to do so, in order that they may gain experience before the time comes for them to be fully responsible for the choices they make. But some find it difficult to treat their grown-up children as people in their own right, entitled to plan their own lives. Sometimes they continue to give unasked-for advice and exert emotional pressure to get them to do as they want.

It is also important to get the right balance between over concern and lack of care. Older teenagers do not want a mother to be yearning over them day and night, even when several hundred miles lie between them. It is damaging to a mother to go on living through her children's lives. It is important, at the time when they leave home, that she has enough to occupy her of a useful, creative and absorbing kind (see chapter 16).

New relationships
In some societies parents do select the marriage partner for their children, but we have very little say in the partners our children choose, however strongly we may feel on the subject. It is unwise to criticize their choices and can be counter-productive. Just as they defended the school friends we disapproved of, so they are likely to stick to their own choice of girl or boyfriend. If your opinion is asked, it may be gently given but, in nearly every case, it is neither right nor effective to try to end a relationship forcibly. Parents have to trust that what

they have taught in earlier years and, ideally, been able to demonstrate in their own relationship together, will have provided patterns to be followed. It is almost always best to welcome the person a son or daughter has chosen. If you don't do so you are also likely to put at risk the closeness of your own relationship with them. Dr Jean Coope, in *Menopause*, advises: 'You may not think the stranger is the perfect son or daughter-in-law, but the chances are that your children know who will suit them better than you do, and the sooner you accept this fact, the happier your family will be.'

Living-in
Many young people take living with a current girl or boyfriend for granted. Parents may feel embarrassed and unsure of how to treat these relationships. There is no protocol to follow and how they decide to handle the matter is a personal decision. It seems to me that parents as well as their children have rights, so if you do not feel comfortable about letting the couple share a bedroom in the family home, you should be free to say so. How you do so is another matter. It never hurts to be gentle and courteous as well as firm. Most children respect genuine moral convictions. They are only likely to be resentful if they suspect that their parents are acting from nothing better than outraged respectability.

When a son or daughter decides to settle down and live with a partner for the foreseeable future, rather than getting married, the situation is different. Parents may have to come to terms with this, and accept the partner, in spite of the many problems such a relationship causes for others in the family. There are no ground rules for knowing how to handle these semi-permanent relationships in the context of the larger family circle. The couple themselves may find it no problem, but Grandpa or Auntie may see it differently. Many of us feel uncomfortable when we do not have a pattern to follow.

Some parents will be very upset, in some cases because it cuts across their genuine convictions. One mother, whose daughter has lived with her boyfriend for about eight years, constantly nags her daughter about getting married and feels deep personal pain and grief. Other parents may be able to accept the situation philosophically. The main point is that we can do nothing to change matters. But it is important that we keep family ties strong. It is possible for both parents and children to show mutual love and respect in spite of their very different views.

Most mothers imagine their children's wedding, but it is sad when a parent puts pressure on her son or daughter to marry. It is important to accept our children, single or married, without making them feel that they are less valued if they remain single, or if they marry someone who is not our choice. When young people remain single, they will be open to pressure from plenty of other people. They need to be able to relax without hints or recriminations from their own parents.

'I'm terrified I'll cry,' a mother confessed before her daughter's wedding. It is obviously an emotional occasion for parents and it is important that they recognize, right from the start, that another person now comes first in their child's love and loyalty. In the trite words of many a wedding speech, they have gained a son or daughter. Whether the family's love is really extended to include the new member, is affected by the parents' reaction. If they have never let their son or daughter go but are still jealously holding on to them, they may resent the marriage partner and therefore look for every possible fault. No one may seem perfect enough for your child but, given the will, it is easy to discover plenty that is good. Since this is the partner chosen by your child, it is vital to be positive and optimistic. When you act in a loving way, the other person is more likely to respond and to show the best side of their nature.

Second time round
Some parents may face disappointment when they find that their child is to marry someone who has been married before and already has children. Mothers who dreamed fondly of a white wedding, a handsome bridegroom and grandchildren soon on the scene, may find that their daughter is planning to marry a man her father's age, who has an ex-wife and some teenage children of his own. Similarly, a son may embark on a marriage with a wife who has her own children. Some children may be willing and glad to talk over beforehand the implications of forming a reconstituted family. Although they can gently put their point of view, parents must then accept the situation. It is worth asking if all our sadness and anxiety is in fact for our child. We should not underestimate the effect of our own disappointment. It is important to recognize and come to terms with these feelings in order to be positive and constructive about the marriage.

Becoming grandparents

Some women scarcely feel the loss of their children, because by the time their youngest is launched, their eldest has a child of his or her own. One mother of six told me that she moved happily from motherhood to grandmotherhood with no time between for mourning the empty nest. Her children all live near, and the house is still full with visiting grandchildren. Other parents long for grandchildren but find that their children delay marriage, or else their career-minded daughters or daughters-in-law have no intention of starting a family for a good few years. I can remember at one time being the only one in a group of women my age who was not able to produce photos and tell anecdotes about grandchildren.

Other women would gladly put off becoming a grandmother, because it makes them feel old. The fact of the matter is that you have no choice either way, and rightly so. It seems inappropriate even to mention your feelings on the subject to your children. They could feel angry, embarrassed and even guilty because of the comments of over-anxious parents who keep hinting about their longing for grandchildren, or make it clear that they think there should be no more. The couple alone have the right to choose what they do and should not be expected to discuss the matter with their parents unless they wish to.

When children do arrive, it is their parents, not their grandparents, who should decide how they are to be brought up. It may be hard to stand by and see your grandchild subjected to what you believe to be wrong methods of mixed feeding, potty training or general discipline, but you have already had your chance to bring up children. There are more ways of showing disapproval than by speaking your mind. Even unspoken criticism can be felt. It is important to support parents and to co-operate as far as you possibly can. A grandparent who tries to counteract parents' own methods by being over-indulgent or strict will only create further problems. What matters most to the child is that he should be treated consistently. The role of grandparents is to give time and unconditional love.

Substitute parents

Grandparents are sometimes left to do much of the child-minding while parents are out at work. There are some situations where this may be necessary and other times when grandparents take over during a crisis. Although every family must make its own plans, it is only fair for grandparents to have freedom of choice in this matter. One or both of them may not wish to cope with parenting a second time round, having not long been released from the exhaustion and limitations of childcare on their own account.

I overheard a conversation between two women, one of whom was talking about her new grandchild. 'I wouldn't mind,' she explained, 'but they just took it for granted that she would go back to work and I would look after the baby, without even asking me.' Even so, she had meekly done as they wished and taken on a responsibility that was clearly a bit of a burden. Naturally, all grandparents will be ready to help in emergencies or in special situations.

Step-grandparents

More and more people these days take on step-grandchildren when their children marry. All new family relationships are delicate and need loving and thoughtful handling. Stepfamilies call for additional sensitivity and unselfish caring on everyone's part. The older generation have greater maturity and insights which they can usefully contribute, even though the situation is not of their making.

. It is not always easy to accept the children of your child's marriage partner, especially if their existence may mean that you are unlikely to have grandchildren of your own. These children may already have grandparents belonging to both their parents, so your role will be a delicate one. One grandmother in this position wrote, 'I thought they were lucky to have me, but they were not grateful at all. They treated me as an intruder.'

Where there is a mix of your own grandchildren and step-grandchildren, it can be hard to be even-handed and learn to accept the new arrivals. In a handbook for step-grandparents the writers advise: 'Try to be fair in all your dealings with the grandchildren, including natural and step-grandchildren together whenever possible. Look for the good in your step-grandchildren and try not to compare them unfavourably with your natural grandchildren. Always let the parents know any suggestions or arrangements you have made with any of the grandchildren.'

Some grandparents have the sadness of losing rather than gaining grandchildren. There are many different ways in which death or divorce can alter the family pattern and there are no ground rules to help us know how to behave, as there are in the case of the traditional nuclear family. Many grandparents in these situations speak of their sense of powerlessness as well as their confusion as they try to sort out their sadness and loss and learn to accept their new families.

All the children involved are likely to have suffered too, and with patience and tact it may be possible to extend love and acceptance to them. Your son or daughter and their new partner will also need your loving acceptance and support. It is pointless· and harmful to hark back to how things used to be, although the conflict of loyalties may be hard to handle. You may be able to continue giving care and support to the abandoned partner but it is still necessary to accept both the loss and the change and to look for a positive way forward.

Acceptance

When our children grow up, we no longer make the decisions for them, but accept the decisions they make for themselves and their own families, and we must do it as constructively and cheerfully as we can. This is the biggest change we need to negotiate. The happiest families are those where parents and children have succeeded in making the transition from a relationship of dependence to one of mutual friendship and sharing. It is no longer our job to criticize or bring pressure to bear. They have as much right to their lives as we have to ours. Once we accept that fact, we can relax and enjoy the relationship, knowing that, because we are not tying them down, they are all the more likely to remain our friends and even to continue to come to us for support and for advice. We may also gain — but not as a right — valued sons and daughters-in-law and grandchildren to love and enjoy.

ACTION CHECKPOINTS

☐ Set your children free.

☐ Make friends with your children.

☐ Live your own life — not your child's.

☐ Look for the best in your child's partner.

☐ Accept your children's decisions.

☐ Enjoy having grandchildren as a privilege — not a right.

SECTION 5
SEX, SINGLENESS AND MARRIAGE

12
SEX IN TODAY'S WORLD

The Things People Say

'A person who is not healthy sexually is not a healthy person.'
American sex therapist

'The other destructive myth in our lives is that sexual activity is natural, while sexual inactivity is not.'
Celia Haddon, author of *The Limits of Sex*

'A man's sexuality is an incredibly fragile thing.'
Koo Stark, photographer

'Sex is important to everybody but I think it's been blown up into a thing that you must have and do.'
Barbara Cartland, novelist

'I've had a very long and happy life without sex. I know many women can live without it.'
Rosemary Anne Sisson, writer

'I think we do exaggerate the importance of sex. . . Long periods of chastity are perfectly OK, particularly when you are working hard. I also think a promiscuous woman is very unlikely to be a happy woman.'
Tina Brown, editor of *Vanity Fair*

'It seems that not only are you supposed to enjoy sex, but you're supposed to talk about how much you enjoy it. That I find tiresome, I must say.'
Doris Saatchi, art collector

'One of the effects of media exploitation is that sexual intercourse has lost its moral mystique. The moment of penetration no longer has the aura of an earth-shaking moral event in a person's life. Technique has replaced morality as the crucial question to ask about sex.'
Lewis Smedes, *Sex in the Real World*

Men and women who are now in their forties and fifties grew up in a society that had been first shocked, then revolutionized by the 'revelations' of American sex researcher Alfred Kinsey. Masters and Johnson followed in his steps, conducting laboratory experiments into human sexual behaviour. The achievements of their monitored sexual athletes led them to prescribe standards of sexual behaviour which were quite unrealistic in terms of ordinary people living normal lives. So it became necessary to provide therapy for those unable to achieve the same kind of performance. Sex manuals and sex therapists soon flooded the market to help people make the grade. At around the same time the advent of the contraceptive pill gave women freedom from the fear of pregnancy. So the age of unlimited and uninhibited sex was underway.

In her book, *The Limits of Sex*, Celia Haddon describes how claims for the value and importance of physical sex became ever more extravagant. In 1970 one psychologist stated that 'an active and rewarding sex life. . . is indispensable if one is to achieve his full potential as a member of the human race.' Dr Alex Comfort lifted the argument to the realm of world peace when he maintained that sexual activity of every kind is necessary in order to free human beings from the instinct to fight and harm others. He insisted that the world is run by powerful but sick people who control others because they have failed to eroticize their experience in a harmless way.

A wide range of so-called sexual sicknesses was diagnosed. Instead of masturbation being classified as wrong or harmful, as it had been in Victorian times, it became not only permissible but obligatory by the new standards. In the US, women were treated for 'masturbatory orgasmic inadequacy,' which would be laughable if it were not both sad and harmfully misleading. The sexual revolution, which was thought to free people from feelings of sexual guilt, gave reasons for experiencing a whole new kind of guilt. The old standards were turned on their heads. Teenagers began to feel ashamed, not of having sex, but of remaining virgins, while older women felt pressured by the necessity to have multiple orgasms of the right kind and frequency. Celia Haddon comments, 'There is something for everyone to worry about.'

One sad aspect of the sexual revolution is the fact that by and large the churches have had little to contribute that is positive and constructive. Some churchmen have gone along with the new permissiveness by conceding that as long as two people love each other that is all that really matters. Too few senior church leaders have been prepared publicly to state that sex outside marriage, as well as homosexual practice, are viewed in biblical teaching as outside God's will and purpose for human good. Christians have also failed to care sufficiently for the victims of the new morality, or to demonstrate a satisfying alternative in positive, healthy family life.

Now that help is urgently needed to stem the threatened spread of AIDS, some governments are looking to the churches to put forward a limiting view of sex. This is ironic, but at least provides another chance to do some hard and honest thinking, in the light of Jesus' teaching, to provide positive Christian guidelines for sex and marriage. At the same time Christians are committed to caring and compassionate action to help those who are homosexual, and all who suffer from AIDS or any sexually transmitted disease.

A Christian view of sex

Biblical Christian thinking does not isolate genital sex and its pleasurable effects from the human relationship involved. Physical sex is one aspect of the total loving relationship between a man and woman. Much secular thinking puts the same emphasis on the whole relationship, but the teaching of Jesus and the New Testament goes further. It states that sex is not appropriate in every situation where a couple are mutually attracted, or even within a relationship that is expected to last for some months or even years. The only valid context for physical sex is marriage, by which is meant a permanent relationship, publicly acknowledged and entered into with mutual promises. Within marriage, sex is viewed as necessary, enjoyable and good.

Such narrow boundaries for the expression of physical sex may seem unrealistic and even crippling in a society which is obsessed with sex. But in rescuing sex from unrestricted genital expression, this belief sets men and women free to enjoy their sexuality in a fuller and deeper way. Much of the mutual enjoyment of the other sex is lost if the only end in view, for at least one of the two, is to get the other into bed at the first opportunity. Instead of making sex a better and richer experience, current 'freedoms' have impoverished it. In fact, men and women are often no longer free to explore and share the many aspects of maleness and femaleness which add texture, richness and depth to work and leisure life. Women who find that homosexual men make wonderful friends, may be reflecting the fact that the freedom from preoccupation with physical sex leaves the relationship wide open to a full range of shared experiences which should be enjoyed freely between heterosexual men and women too.

Celibacy

According to the Christian view, celibacy and marriage are equally valuable. Chastity is the virtue either of keeping sex for marriage or of abstaining from sex altogether. People who are celibate do not belong to a kind of neuter gender because they do not practise physical sex. They are still open to appreciate and enjoy every aspect of sexuality and of the relationship between the sexes, other than a genital one. Many celibate people who have not invested their love in one other human being, have a wealth of creative love and care to give to the world. In return, they often experience a depth of love not known to the non-celibate. Not all such people live within religious orders. Jesus taught that some of his followers would willingly forego a life of sexual activity in order to fulfil their special work for him in the world. As well as those who have deliberately given up all idea of marriage for the sake of their Christian calling, there are others who fail to find a marriage partner and accept that situation as part of God's plan for their life.

One religious who responded to God's calling to celibacy explained: 'Chastity does not consist of deadening our heart but rather in giving it a liberty of love, a single aim, a transparency to God. Our chastity, indeed our whole life, only makes sense in relation to our love to God. . . I doubt whether I should ever have experienced such wealth and depth of love, from and for so many, had I not followed. . . my vocation.'

Sex and religion are not alternative outlets. Married as well as celibate people are able to experience the love of God which can transform and enrich sexuality beyond the ecstasy of physical sex. It is not easy to exercise sexual self-control in our society. Celia Haddon suggests that the celibate and the single are the nonconformists of our day. Even when their attitude to chastity is positive and enriching, they are still made to feel that they are less than normal and lacking what it takes to be fully developed human beings.

Christians believe not only in celibacy outside marriage, but chastity, or faithfulness, within it. Sexual acts outside marriage are wrong, whether between those of opposite or the same sex. In defining these limits, Christians are trying to carry out the pattern laid down by God, who created our sexuality. The basis of this understanding of marriage is laid down in the very first

144

book of the Bible: 'That is why a man leaves his father and mother and is united with his wife, and they become one.' Jesus quoted these words in his own teaching about marriage. The permanent, publicly acknowledged relationship of marriage is the only happy and safe environment for full sexual experience. Within marriage there is room for sex to flourish in an atmosphere of mutual commitment, trust and security. In following his guidelines Christians believe that they are in no way impoverishing human nature or divesting sex of its importance but are putting it into its proper sphere, where it can be enjoyed with mutual benefit and with no tragic side-effects. Many of the deeply painful and depersonalizing situations in our society come about as the direct result of a broader but lower valuation of sex and sexual relationships.

Sex and midlife

At the menopause a woman reaches the end of her childbearing years. But this does not signify the end of her sexual life. Some women are worried that once they are past the age for having children, they will stop enjoying sex. Some may even feel that perhaps sex is not quite right if it has nothing to do with procreation. Women who have valued the sex act just because of its potential to create a child may find that it no longer gives them pleasure. But that will be for psychological rather than physiological reasons.

Sex is important in marriage for more reasons than the begetting of children. It expresses love and strengthens unity as well as being the supreme way of renewing commitment and of giving and receiving pleasure. There is every reason why it should continue to be pleasurable and satisfying for both husband and wife for the rest of their married life. Once the fear of unwanted pregnancy is past there is greater freedom to enjoy it.

Men in midlife

Although there is no reason why middle age should mean a lessening of sexual potency in men, some do complain of a decline in sexual ability in midlife. Almost always the causes are psychological rather than physical or hormonal (see chapter 2). Certain drugs given for some other disorder may cause temporary impotence, so that is something to check with the doctor. Sometimes fear of a heart attack inhibits sexual performance. More often the cause is loss of confidence or extreme pressure of work. Discovering the reason for the temporary loss of libido and keeping the whole problem in perspective will help.

An understanding and patient wife can do a great deal to help. It is important for her to give her husband confidence in any area of his life, as well as on the sexual level. When they make love, she can help by being patient and relaxed as well as responsive to any shared physical closeness, rather than increasing his anxiety to 'perform' satisfactorily.

Coping with problems

During the menopause a drop in hormone levels may account for a temporary loss of sexual desire in women, but this need not be more than a passing loss. General feelings of being under the weather and slight depression can all combine to make sex seem uninteresting or just a necessary chore! Frequent periods and heavy bleeding may be further non-inducements to regular sex. It is important to realize that this state of affairs is only temporary and that sex may become even more exciting and rewarding once the menopause has passed.

After the menopause the vagina becomes drier and less elastic, so husbands may need to be a bit more gentle, especially at first, and a little more persevering. When partners are more or less the same age, this slower response will be balanced by the older man's more delayed reactions. But before the two adapt to a slightly changed but often more fully satisfying sex life, there can be temporary hitches. The wife's reluctance or the husband's loss of libido may cause disappointment and frustration and a temporary lull in sex. Sometimes the couple may allow the physical side of their relationship to fade out altogether. For others it may become infrequent for a number of reasons, such as:

- chronic tiredness

- overfull lives

- unresolved resentments

- loss of confidence leading to loss of libido

- inhibitions through teenagers or parents sharing the house

- temporary hormone imbalance in wife

- boredom

'No sex, please?'

When there is a low level of sexual drive in one or other partner, it is easy for the couple to drift into no sex. This is probably not a planned strategy, but the result of constant tiredness, busy programmes or some of the physical discomforts or psychological problems already mentioned. It is at this stage that a couple sometimes decide to change to separate beds or even separate rooms. This may be a perfectly sensible decision based on the fact that one partner snores, or one sleeps poorly and wants to read or listen to the radio without disturbing the other. But it does mean that there is little chance for physical closeness or the impulse cuddling that can say so much in its own right, as well as leading naturally and delightfully to full sexual enjoyment.

There is no reason why a couple should continue to have sex into old age if they decide together that they do not want to, but it is important that they make a decision rather than lapse into no sex as a result of neglect or unresolved problems. The implications of such a decision need to be thought out. First, it must be the right course for both of them. Marriage is a loving, caring relationship where each thinks of the other's good and this is especially important in relation to sex. If one partner still feels the desire for sex, then a way should be found to meet that need, with unselfish giving as well as restraint as each tries to satisfy the other. Even when both decide that sex is no longer a necessary ingredient of the marriage, close physical contact should not cease. Our bodies are part of our whole makeup and the intimate relationship of marriage needs expression in closeness of body as well as of mind and spirit.

Physical closeness brings comfort and reassurance and can ease some of the difficulties and pains of this stage of life as well as helping the couple to stay close in every other way. It is important to make time for such intimacy, as it is an enduring part of marriage. For couples finding full sexual orgasm or satisfying sex hard to achieve, loving physical closeness and touching are also important. Sex therapy for such couples often consists of first learning to be close without trying to climax, so that trust and confidence can be re-established without the tension and pressure of having to achieve. One of the distressing side-effects of the sexual revolution has been the emphasis on successful sexual performance. Those who cannot measure up to text-book success may feel a sense of guilt or failure. But within the security and time-scale of marriage, partners can be free to express their love physically as they can and will, without pressure to meet required standards. Technique is not the most important issue.

It is sad when boredom is the reason for married couples losing interest in sex. Dr Brice Pitt comments in *Making the Most of Middle Age*: 'So much publicity is now given to the art of making love, what men and women need from each other, and how to please your partner, that there is little excuse for a dull, unimaginative sex life even in the supposedly stolid middle-aged.' Consulting sex manuals might help, but one of the benefits of having been married a number of years should be a deeper understanding of your partner and of what will give pleasure. Variety is the spice of life even — or especially — where sex is concerned. Try to break the mould of same-time, same-place, same-routine sex.

Sex cannot be switched on to order within a marriage. Where there are deep resentments and unresolved areas of anger or plain misunderstanding, the sexual relationship — if it's an honest one — will suffer too.

Sex and the single person
Many people now reaching forty plus, have been enjoying a full sex life as a single person. Some have expected to sleep with anyone they fancied who treated them to a night out — or, in the case of a man, expected bed for the night in return for dinner. Others may have had a succession of live-in boy or girl friends, lasting as long as it suited them both. Others may have maintained a long-term extra-marital affair.

This kind of no-strings-attached use of sex seems to combine the best of both worlds, leaving a woman free to pursue her career and a man unshackled by the commitments of a heavy mortgage and all the other responsibilities that go with a family. But at midlife there are certain realities to be faced. Many may have discovered that the trouble-free lifestyle they had planned has turned out to be a good bit less well-regulated and tidy than they had expected or intended it to be.

Human relationships cannot usually be kept within neat bounds by both partners, but tend to spill over in deep emotions of pain and anger. The bond that accompanies sexual pairing is real and strong and when two people who have been bonded in this way break up, one at least may feel great grief and hurt.

One psychotherapist commented: 'Sex for singles sounds good and I won't even say that it is not sometimes, but I hear the other side when people talk to me. I pick up all the casualties.

Many start off with high hopes but there is a lot of hurt. Many of them go on to wonder if they could ever make a marriage. They begin to doubt their ability to stick at a relationship.'

Even the successful entrepreneurs in sex may have doubts at midlife. Women in particular may realize that the kind of relationships they have enjoyed are less likely to come their way once they reach middle age. That stage cannot be put off for ever. They have no partner with whom to face middle or old age, or who will provide stability and companionship when they need it. Even the least maternal may begin to regret having had no child.

Tina Brown, editor of *Vanity Fair*, says, 'What no one really explained to women, as they went out on their feminist forays, was that they were giving up something. What are tragic to behold are women. . . who suddenly do a volte face at fifty and say, "Why didn't I have children?" . . . And I think the regret comes because they wanted everything. . . but you can't expect to have everything at once.'

Some who are still young enough plan a baby without a husband, but the cost to the mother will be high and the cost to the child, who has no choice in the matter, may be even higher.

Single people who have remained celibate also face the fact that they will not now have children. One counsellor described the feelings of some single women at midlife who come to her, unable to understand their renewed anguish. Often they say, 'I thought that I had been through all this and settled it in my mind ten years ago, yet here I am having to come to terms with the same issue all over again.' Her reply is, 'You are not going back on something you finished with. You sorted it out and settled it ten years ago, but now you are facing it as a new problem at your present age. There is no failure because you have to work it through in a new way at forty or fifty.'

Single people, whether celibate or not, may also be plagued by doubts as to whether they would have been capable of sustaining a relationship in marriage. Added to that, they bear the burden of society's thumbs down. Celia Haddon comments: 'Those who are celibate, particularly those who have celibacy forced upon them, often feel outcast, anxious and ashamed.' But those who are courageous enough to face their singleness and their feelings honestly are free to discover, in the words of a Roman Catholic priest, that celibacy 'is not a matter of uprooting sexuality but of becoming sexual in a different way. Sexuality, for the celibate as well, remains a wonderful gift of God, given because he loves us so.'

Homosexuals may also fear loneliness in old age, whether they have had a physical relationship or not. Bishop Jim Thompson, in *Half Way*, comments: 'The homosexual who has never had a physical relationship, because of religious conviction, or fear, or lack of opportunity, can be subject to the same panic in midlife as the heterosexual spinster or bachelor. There can be the desperate feeling that life has passed them by, and they stand on a precipice, wondering whether to jump into the arms of the first person who offers, or risk endless loneliness.'

He goes on to advise those still wrestling with uncertainty, 'He or she ought to examine, with the help of others, what his or her own attitudes to sexuality really are. If there is no one to talk it through with, then there is the real risk of hopeless adventure. It is more helpful to meet real people who have come to terms with their lives, than to wander around lost and alone in a maze of fantasies. Solutions will not be discovered in solitary confinement.'

The spread of AIDS may have signalled the end of the gigantic sex trip that has been going on since the sixties. There is more chance that those who have an alternative and more satisfying philosophy of sex may now speak up and be heard. There is also the chance to put an alternative belief into practice.

ACTION CHECKPOINT

☐ Take a fresh look at your views of sex. Do they need revising?

13
MARRIAGE IN MIDLIFE

The Things People Say

'I think marriage can be a very good basis for developing your own personality, provided you feel that is something of value to do and not just selfish. I think some people do think that is selfish and that marriage is about bringing up a family and looking after the house.'
Marriage counsellor

'When you are in a relationship in which you ask each other's advice, when you respect each other, then the outward image of success, who earns the money, doesn't matter.'
Esther Rantzen, television presenter

'Many people who get divorced don't find anything better and really wish they hadn't. . . I think this whole thing of racing off to get divorced at the first snag you hit seems pathetic.'
Tina Brown, editor, *Vanity Fair*

'Everything in this century has been put on the marital couple. It's asked to sustain an enormous amount of emotional intensity, which it probably wasn't asked to do before, and that's hard. I think that's partly the problem, and the prospect of sustaining this for forty or fifty years. It's an awful lot to bear.'
Juliet Mitchell-Rossdale, psychoanalyst, author, feminist

'Marriage gets better the longer you're married!'
One of my favourite aunts

'Self-absorbed family life, and a self-absorbed marriage, sacrifice the true selves and potential of the people involved.'
Bishop Jim Thompson, *Half Way*

'The couple contract must be renegotiated in midlife.'
Gail Sheehy, *Passages*

Now that men and women live longer, many people suggest that it is unrealistic to expect to sustain one marriage for a lifetime. After all, they point out, that could involve living together for fifty or sixty years, compared to the twenty or thirty of previous generations. They argue that since human beings change they are going to need a different kind of partner in order to find fulfilment and satisfaction for the whole of their lives. By this definition, marriage is an arrangement that should be terminated once it no longer meets the needs of one or other of the partners.

Gail Sheehy defines the journey into midlife as a transition from accepting the authority and beliefs of others to defining and recognizing one's own values and judgement. She sees the person who successfully survives the hazards of the middle years becoming someone in their own right who is not afraid to take responsibility and to admit to 'what I really feel'. She accepts that such a change may drastically affect relations with a marriage partner. Her advice is, 'Let it happen to you. Let it happen to your partner. Let the feelings. Let the changes.' But there are many people who would not find it fulfilling to be themselves at any cost and at the expense of another. The Christian life-style, with its emphasis on the happiness and well-being of others, also brings fulfilment and can yield deeper satisfaction than the wholehearted pursuit of personal ends.

Walking out on your partner may not be the answer to midlife change and you may not want a divorce, but you are likely to find that you need to update your relationship if the marriage is to be sound and mutually satisfying for another twenty or thirty years. Just as individuals need to take stock at this stage, in order to lay the ghosts of the past, grapple with the present and set new goals for the future, so a couple may need to reappraise their marriage in those same areas.

It's easy to be aware that things need sorting out but to be too preoccupied with the routine of living to do anything about it. It is important to stop and talk. Some couples make a habit of talking through whatever is bothering either of them whenever it crops up. Others who put off the evil day may find it helps to book a weekend away together so that there is time to talk and listen to each other and sort matters out. Failing that, plan a day out together or even spend an evening with the television off, and concentrate on each other and discuss your feelings and needs honestly. This may all seem a bit of an unnecessary fuss, but it's a small price to pay in time and trouble and money in order to save the marriage and turn it into an asset rather than a liability. Too often relationships go sour or become impoverished through lack of attention.

Individuals survive the shake-up of midlife change and often emerge from it stronger and invigorated. A marriage can do the same, provided the couple are prepared to talk things through and really want to make a go of it. They must also want to please each other and help each other to find fulfilment, as well as looking for personal satisfaction. Total selfishness is a killer in any relationship.

Expectations in marriage

Many people who get married have unreal expectations of marriage in general. Sometimes their concept is based on the kind of relationship their parents had. A young wife may assume that her husband will come shopping with her and he may take it for granted that she will stay at home while he goes to the local football match, or plays golf with the boys. Each may have a completely different attitude from the other on the subject of husband and wife roles, money, children and the family. Because neither has examined or thought out their views, or the reasons why they hold them, there is serious misunderstanding when attitudes and behaviour clash. As time goes on, there is unwilling acceptance of each other, which may be good-humoured, but which can also hide a great deal of anger and resentment.

Other couples have unreal expectations of their particular partner. One marriage counsellor commented, 'It is a common difficulty that couples want too much from each other. You can't expect one person to satisfy all your needs.'

Older or maturer couples may face marriage more realistically and discuss their expectations before they marry, even laying down guidelines to be jointly agreed and accepted. One wife, who has now returned part-time to her own career while she cares for their two small children, accepted before marrying that her high-powered executive husband would not give any help in the house. She willingly agreed within the context of all the other benefits the marriage would bring. Because her expectations were realistic, she accepts without rancour the fact that she must either do the work herself or employ someone to do it for her. Obviously, no loving couple will present each other with a hard and fast ultimatum but will try to work through together what each can reasonably give to the partnership.

In midlife many areas need to be tackled afresh in this way. For most couples, circumstances will differ radically from the early days of marriage. The household may now consist of several teenagers or an elderly relative. If one partner opts out of the physical caring, decision-making and adolescent crises at the expense of the other, a load of resentment and dissatisfaction soon builds up. Honest discussion is needed about the new demands and problems to be faced.

It is not only the partner bearing the heavy end of the load who may feel aggrieved. A husband who has a demanding job, and is used to returning home to find dinner ready to be put on the table, may be distinctly put out if his wife is upstairs helping his mother-in-law onto the commode instead. He will probably feel even more hard done by if she is not yet back from her new job.

New situations call for a reassessment of roles within the marriage. It is better to discuss realistically what each can expect from the other and how both can contribute to the good of the partnership, before major new changes are made. Human beings are infinitely flexible and able to adjust when survival depends on it.

The new balance of power may not suit both partners ideally. Few compromises are perfect. But if each can be honest about themselves, try to understand the other, and be ready to give as well as take, they will be able to capitalize on all the benefits of facing life together as a stable and mature couple, for the second half of their journey.

Talking it through

Many of us have glanced across at a middle-aged couple sitting at a nearby table in a restaurant and noticed their complete lack of communication. Of course, companionable silence can be one of the more pleasurable experiences of intimacy, but that kind of silence has a very different look to it. Courtship is marked by a compulsive desire to share everything about yourself with the person you love, and marriage usually begins the same way. Somewhere along the line, real communication can break down and talking together dwindle to basic exchanges about the practical commonplaces of daily life — 'Did you remember to post the letters?' — 'Will you pick up Auntie?' The things that really matter — personal hopes, fears, ambitions, deep joys and sadnesses — are locked away out of sight.

Both partners may have tried to talk at a more intimate level but found that the other one was not listening. This can happen in both directions. A wife can be busy bringing up a family and so taken up with their affairs that she fails to give her husband real attention. She cannot guess at his anxieties or burdens because she has never encouraged him to talk about them or found time to stop whatever she was doing and listen. Husbands, in turn, may not listen to their wives.

One career wife spoke about her exasperation when her husband listened to her with half an ear as he watched television. 'I know he's tired out and that's the way he relaxes, but I long to switch the television off and make him listen to me,' she complained. She needed more than a non-committal grunt in answer to her outpourings. Listening involves hearing what is left unsaid as well as the words actually spoken and to hear in that way requires the sort of attention that, sadly, we may rarely offer to our own nearest and dearest.

Some couples who have failed to hear what the other has been saying over a number of years may need the help of a third person, probably a trained counsellor, to get them talking again. Such a person acts as a catalyst, providing the right opportunity and atmosphere for each to express honestly what their feelings are about themselves and each other. Counsellors find that husband and wife are often amazed to discover what the other is actually thinking. Although they have been living together for years they have had no idea how the other really felt. Some harbour resentments going back many years, which only come to the surface when a crisis causes the couple to come for counselling. A good counsellor helps them to interpret the meaning behind the words each speaks.

Within the familiarity of marriage there are many subtle ways of showing anger, contempt or cruelty. Because none of these emotions is overtly expressed it is always possible for the offending partner to act the innocent and deny any hidden meaning. But tone of voice, studied indifference, or an apparently harmless question may carry a weight of meaning based on years of sniping and criticism. Sometimes one partner suspects hidden meanings which were genuinely not intended.

The counsellors' job is to help the couple to sort out what really lies behind the words as well as the actions. They may ask the husband to say how he feels, then question the wife about that answer, checking with him if she has understood his meaning in the right way. Gradually they hope to strip away the disguises and help both partners to understand themselves and each other better and recognize the ways in which they interact.

Failure to take account of the other's feelings can sometimes result from plain ignorance of the facts. A man who is made redundant may feel unable to tell his wife what has happened and keep up the pretence of leaving for work every day. She cannot show consideration when she doesn't know what's the matter. Lack of imagination may also prevent one partner from recognizing what the other is coping with. A husband who tells his wife about his redundancy does not always meet with the right kind of sympathy or support. Because he cannot put into words the pain and loss of confidence he is suffering, she fails to recognize his distress. It may be that one partner is so involved with their own painful feelings during the experiences of midlife, that there is no room for the other's needs.

One marriage counsellor described her occasional use of role reversal. Halfway through a session she invites husband and wife to change chairs and pretend to be each other. She then asks what kind of day each has had, telling them to answer as if they were the other. It is surprising how little each knows, even about the other's daily routine or the regular demands and pressures involved.

Awareness and understanding can help but, unless both genuinely have the other's interests as well as their own at heart, it will not automatically improve the marriage. If a marriage is to survive, self-sacrifice as well as self-fulfilment must be the keynote. Many women have seen a new and demanding career at midlife as their way to satisfaction, only to find that it becomes a prime cause of problems for their husband. While it is not right that either partner should always have to give way to the other, each may have to concede at times, for both their sakes and for the well-being of their marriage.

Changed patterns

Some of the changes and crises of midlife can easily become crises for the marriage too. A marriage that is stable and good will survive some rocking of the boat but, if the relationship is not soundly based, any new factor can threaten to sink it. It is likely that the roles of husband and wife were defined early on in marriage. Now, if the children have grown up and the wife wishes to embark on a career, or return to her former one, or if an elderly relative needs to receive full-time care, the roles may need to be redefined.

It is no good for a wife to initiate changes that will affect both partners before talking things over thoroughly with her husband. Provided both are prepared to give some ground it is possible to sort out roles afresh and to plan new patterns for the marriage. A man who, through choice or redundancy, decides to work from home, may be willing to take on simple cooking and housework so that his wife can return to full-time employment. He will usually benefit from knowing that there will still be one regular wage coming in.

Talking through the advantages and the snags, and deciding what each can reasonably expect from the other, should reduce the threat of future rows and recriminations. If a wife is going to be out all day and her husband refuses to help in the home, she may have to consider arranging or paying for help if she can afford to — in order to do what she wants to do. If she will be earning, that will eat into her profits, but she is likely to be more contented than if she had given up her job. And the marriage is likely to be far happier than if she is working flat out while she is at home and blaming her husband for giving her no help.

When an elderly relative is to be cared for, it is important that having some time off together should be top priority for the couple. The marriage is still of prime importance.

If a husband wishes to set up his own business, his wife should think through the implications of having her husband at home all day, if she is at home too. Being together night and day can put a new kind of pressure on the relationship, particularly at first. But, wisely handled and prepared for, it can enrich the marriage. Talking to others whose judgement can be trusted, and who have weathered the same kind of changes, may be a help.

New beginnings

Midlife is a time to come to terms with the past so that the future can be faced with no unfinished business to block the way ahead. Married couples need to work through their shared past disappointments and mistakes as much as individuals do. 'I'll never forget the time you. . . ' can be an aggrieved refrain in real marriages as well as in music-hall jokes.

Many couples retain their sense of injury — or perceived injury — at the hands of the other, for many years. They may refer to it or harbour it secretly and allow it to sour their trust and love. If a marriage is to survive as a healthy and beneficial partnership for the second half of life, these remembered wrongs must be dealt with. They must be forgiven and not left in limbo, ready to be recalled if needed for attack or defence. Accepting forgiveness can be hard too. Serious wrongs — unfaithfulness, cruelty of one kind or another — are not easy to confess or to forgive, but any other way of dealing with the past will harm not only the marriage but the two individuals — whether they need to forgive or to be forgiven.

Affairs

Some manuals on sex and marriage recommend an affair as a means of refreshing a stale marriage. Men and women who grew up during the swinging sixties may have a different view of sexual fidelity from those who are slightly older. But, however much people may defend the extra-marital affair in theory, many still discover in practice that their partner's unfaithfulness leaves them feeling deeply betrayed. A number of marriage counsellors I have spoken to all agree that they have never in fact come across a case where infidelity *has* improved a marriage. Instead, they all found that adultery — alone among the changes within marriage — was perceived as the ultimate betrayal. A wife whose husband had taken a girl out on a number of occasions would tell the counsellor, 'This time it's different — they've slept together.'

Lewis Smedes, in his book *Sex in the Real World*, lists a number of reasons why adultery is so much more common now than in previous generations. He also suggests why, nonetheless, it is still perceived as a serious betrayal of the marriage. Not only is it a way of cheating on the partner, and likely to hurt at least one of the three people involved, but it causes damage that goes deep.

'The wrongness of adultery,' he writes, 'is knit into the inner lining of sexuality. Sexual intercourse has a mystique about it: there is something inescapably — if invisibly — special in this encounter. Most people, I suspect, still sense this, even when they do not honour it in practice. Most people who have sex outside marriage still find it necessary to invoke some powerful excuse for it — even to themselves. . . Even if we can convince ourselves that nobody is getting hurt, even if we are sure we are not cheating, we have a suspicion that it is inappropriate.'

There seems to be some reaction against permissiveness within marriage even in sophisticated, secular circles. In an article in the magazine *Options*, Rose Shepherd debunked the glamour surrounding extra-marital affairs and described the downward spiral of personal unhappiness, as well as the destruction of the marriage. Her friend, Miriam, had embarked on what she euphemistically described as 'a wonderful adventure' — her first act of adultery, after a nine-year marriage rooted in mutual devotion and trust.

'Here is the scenario as I envisage it,' Rose Shepherd writes. 'The time has come when she was ripe to take a lover — she had spent so long being, or playing, the devoted wife and mother. John was taking her for granted, so were the children. No one ever said they liked her hair that way, or that she looked lovely when she smiled. . . She wasn't twenty-one any more, and for most of us that is a terrible hardship. . . Miriam's self-confidence needed a boost. . . Then there was the opportunity. She had given up work to have the children and she'd seen them through to school age, when she'd gone out and found herself another job. And it was at the office. . . that she met the man who said. . . "You're lovely when you smile." It is that man who is now her lover.

'Mr X, Mr Other, is predictably married. He has no plans to leave his wife. He finds Miriam appealing and she holds for him the added attraction of being married and committed herself. She won't be making midnight phone calls, she won't be turning up on his doorstep in the small hours.

'Miriam is merely taking her cue from him when she makes nothing of emotion. She's playing at being the grown woman who knows the rules of the game. . . She is in the grip of infatuation and. . . the odds are that it will lead precisely nowhere; that they — and more probably he — will call the whole thing off. And for Miriam it will be. . . that particular type of hell reserved for faithless wives. . . She will have to contain her emotion. . . otherwise John will guess the reason why. So much, then, for their enriched marriage!'

Rose Shepherd goes on to argue that a first affair, usually based on attraction, leads to further affairs based on nothing more than boredom, loneliness, resentment, or the need for further boosting of confidence once the first extramarital partner has bowed out. With the 'lowering of personal standards' that accompanied the first affair, the warning bells are beginning to sound. There may be interludes of excitement or even ecstasy but, for the marriage, there is everything to lose.

What are the options?

Psychiatrist John White suggests that no marriage is problem-free but that there are three options open for dealing with a troubled marriage.

One is to stay together and live 'to make each other miserable, a habit which sometimes becomes too strong to break.' Such self-defeating relationships are less common now, he suggests, and probably restricted to older couples.

The second option is separation or divorce with the trauma and pain that inevitably follow.

The third and most positive option is to work together towards a firmer commitment to the marriage.

Dr White believes that the stresses that destroy marriages are as effective for construction as destruction. There must be a willingness, he admits, by both partners to see and acknowledge their own faults and weaknesses and to accept the weaknesses and strengths of the other. Help or counsel may be needed to reach these new insights. His personal experience is that 'God's "no divorce" rule is not harsh, but merciful, in that it has forced us to examine and resolve conflicts and enter a stronger, richer stage of marriage. At the same time, we know that the same mercy can be shown by God to those who have known both divorce and remarriage.'

ACTION CHECKPOINTS

☐ Start talking to each other — honestly.

☐ Start listening to each other — with both ears.

☐ Make time to take stock as a couple.

☐ Sort out the past — forgive and be forgiven.

☐ Get help if you can't sort yourselves out on your own.

☐ Think through the possible effects of change on you both.

☐ Revise your roles in marriage where necessary or helpful.

☐ Let each other change and let your marriage change.

__14__
ALONENESS

The Things People Say

'Being alone wouldn't be so bad if we weren't so heavily bombarded with the idea of the idyllic twosome.'
Anna Raeburn in *Over 21*

'Singles who have worked through singleness at about thirty, often have another crisis at forty.'
Therapist

'"All by myself" can be either a celebration — "I did it all by myself!" — or a lament of loneliness — "I'm all by myself, nobody loves me!" — an appeal for congratulation or for sympathy.'
The Rev. John Stott

'A lot of people who feel desperately lonely are feeling that on account of the sheer selfish, unimaginative attitudes of other people.'
Roy Trevivian, *So You're Lonely*

'The process, the long process of turning loneliness back into aloneness must begin with the realization that it is not wrong to be alone, and that nothing terrible will happen.'
Anonymous male writer

'Singleness for some means freedom and opportunity. . . and for others it means pain. Sometimes the freedom and the pain inter-mingle.'
The Rev. John Stott

'Being alone does not have to be lonely and one doesn't have to be half of anything.'
Anna Raeburn

'There is nothing more difficult than living with one person, whether it's your sister, your brother, your mother, your father, your best friend. There comes a time, after so long, when it seems intolerable to go on.'
Baroness Grimond

'In marriage two sets of ideas, two different kinds of tastes have got to be accommodated. . . more often than not there is a good deal of giving and taking to be done.'
Margaret Evening, *Who Walk Alone*

In our society it is usually taken for granted that to be happy you must have a partner, and that expectation makes it harder to recognize that there can be some real benefits in being alone. Those of us who are constantly surrounded by people, are conscious of an urge to have time on our own that is so strong as to be almost a physical need. Most of us, in fact, would like the ideal compromise, to spend most of our time with others — or one other — and some time on our own. Very few manage to get the balance right for their particular needs. But in spite of the advantage and the necessity of having time to ourselves, most of us would admit that we need our fellow human beings. Solitary confinement is still reckoned to be one of the cruellest sentences that can be handed out to a prisoner.

There is all the difference in the world between being alone from choice and having aloneness forced upon us by situations beyond our control. Some unmarried people in their forties and fifties and others separated, divorced or widowed, find being alone the hardest part of their lot. In order to be with others they must make the running by inviting people round or fixing up an outing. Most of us know that, when we are feeling low, organizing a dinner or even a coffee party can be an enormous effort. Sometimes it seems impossible even to pick up the phone to ring a friend. But often the only alternative may be to stay in, alone, for much of the time.

When it comes to going out and about, not many women, in particular, have the confidence to go to a pub on their own, or sit alone in a restaurant, at the sort of time when couples and foursomes are meeting there together. It may seem over-sensitive to react so negatively to being without partner or friends, and when morale is high a lone person may feel quite self-assured enough to cope in a positive way. But for those who are feeling hurt and bruised by the desertion or death of a husband or partner, or who deeply feel the lack of a partner, bearing the pain and desolation of being alone can be desperately hard.

Plenty of people in midlife who are not alone physically may still be very lonely. Even after many years of marriage, some husbands and wives are completely unable to share with each other the emotions, needs and interests that are closest to their hearts. Those caring for elderly parents who were once also dear friends may no longer find it possible to share their thoughts and interests with them as they have done in the past, and that can make life lonely too.

Roy Trevivian, a former radio presenter, wrote a book, *So You're Lonely*, about his own experience of loneliness. When it seemed that he had everything going for him — prestige, money, wife, family — he suffered serious depression and mental breakdown. During this period he entered the depths and the bitterness of being alone. He had given up his job, left his wife and family and been stripped bare of all support. He writes about the physical pain of loneliness which he lived with night and day. He went to sleep with pain and woke with it next morning.

He writes: 'Gradually, through the pain of loneliness a light began to dawn. The faintest, smallest flicker of a dawn. In "the world" I was a nobody. . . there were now no props to bolster up a me that needed only props. There was only me and Jesus. . . He didn't take the pain away. He never has completely. . . In spite of the pain, though, I know that I am me and he is Jesus. If losing the pain means losing him, then I'll keep the pain.'

Trevivian continues, 'To go into aloneness without Jesus could drive a person mad and even to suicide. Don't seek aloneness unless you enter that with him. . . I have known people who have gone into loneliness and on into aloneness without him, and as far as this life is concerned "they" have ceased to exist, even though their bodies have stayed alive. However, with him, it is in aloneness that the real treasures lie. You will find him in a way that otherwise you would not. You will find what it is to be a real human being.'

Singleness

Some single women, with successful careers, high incomes and plenty of men and women friends, may be the envy of their married sisters. But a great many ordinary men and women who reach midlife without marrying are made to feel as if they are failures. Often they have to put up with other people's personal comments on the subject. Margaret Clarkson, in her book *Single*, writes, 'The person who marries late or not at all is considered an oddity, not quite normal. Sexual aberrations may be suspected, even hinted at. People feel free to question, to tease, to make sick jokes about being single as they would dare to do about no other personal matter. . . Eventually many of us come to believe that we must be some sort of misfit or we would have married. We struggle increasingly for a sense of identity and self-esteem.'

Another writer on the same subject has had a different experience. She finds that friends and colleagues are too embarrassed to discuss the subject. They seem uncertain if the single person is putting on a good front or has willingly accepted or even chosen singleness. Society's verdict creates real problems for the single person, yet, as one single woman commented, she had found no counsellors to help single people in the way they do married couples.

There are roughly equal numbers of men and women in our society so it could be taken for granted that anyone who wants to get married is able to do so. But there is no guarantee that a suitable partner will conveniently turn up in the right place and at the right time. Some single people who don't find a partner to suit them have the good sense to stay single. They realize that marriage for its own sake will create more problems than it solves. But it takes courage to run counter to popular expectations, to resist the pressure of family and friends and to remain single. One person said, 'My daughter decided not to marry although she had several chances to do so. But she openly admits that she is lonely and that if anyone asked her now, she would be tempted to say yes for the wrong reasons.' It is no easier for men than for women.

On the positive side, single people have many advantages. They are often far freer to choose how they will use their time for their own enjoyment and for others. In our society we encourage women to find personal fulfilment and success by combining marriage and a family with a career and social life of their own. In theory this may be fine but in practice the cost can be high in terms of chronic tiredness, tensions and even a sense of guilt. Most of us have a limited supply of emotional energy to give out and while some women may cut back on commitment to their job, others who respond generously to the demands made upon them at work may come home too tired to meet the emotional needs of husband or children.

A single woman caring for an elderly relative may be in a similar position, but normally the unmarried person is free from the tension that conflicting demands on limited energies can often produce. Single men probably have more to do than those with a wife to superintend the household, but they are still free from the heavy commitments of family life.

As well as being able to give themselves fully and whole-heartedly to their job and their friends, single people are free to make their own choices. They may go on a diet, join the tennis club, watch a particular television programme or take a holiday where they most wish to go. They are free to entertain in their own right and to give time to the people they would like to befriend. Margaret Clarkson, in *Single*, writes, 'Within the limits of Christian behaviour, good taste and thoughtfulness for others, I am free to be myself. I have no need to conform to others' ideas of what I should be.'

An even more important asset of singleness is the opportunity it offers a man or woman to come to terms with the essential solitariness of the human lot. The happily married man or woman may be shielded from the inescapable fact which we all have to face sooner or later — that at the most important moments of life we stand on our own. Above all, at death, we take the unknown journey alone.

The American journalist, Gail Sheehy, describes her reaction to a brush with death when, at the age of thirty-five, she was covering an assignment in Northern Ireland. 'A powerful idea took hold of me,' she writes in *Passages*. 'No one is with me. No one can keep me safe. There is no one who won't ever leave me alone.'

None of us likes to come up hard against this kind of realization. We prefer to have another human being to lean on, to keep us company and to shield us from the knowledge that sooner or later we must be on our own. Married people often shelter under the safe togetherness each partner provides and delay the discovery of their separateness until the relationship is ended by desertion or death. Then they have to learn how to stand alone at a time when they are already under enormous emotional stress and pain. Some do not learn the lesson even then, but continue to be emotional cripples for the rest of their lives, depending on children or friends to supply the strength and decision-making which their partner had previously provided. Single people often learn through necessity to stand alone, to find resources within themselves for dealing with hard decisions and difficult actions.

The fortunate ones discover the truth that Roy Trevivian experienced. It is true that every one of us must finally face utter aloneness, but Jesus offers us his company. When he lived as a man on earth, he experienced loneliness to the limits, so he understands how we feel. He promised his followers that he would be with them to the very end. And St Paul triumphantly asserted that nothing in the whole universe — not life, not death itself — could separate us from God's love in Jesus.

Divorce

Divorce is probably the most traumatic way in which a man or woman can find themselves alone.

'Sometimes I feel that I don't fit into any category,' one divorced woman explained. 'I'm neither single, nor married with a husband. I have good friendships with single women but, when they go off at holiday time, I can't. I have my children. Somehow, because there is still a husband somewhere in the past, they don't think of me as being eligible to join them. My married friends have their own husbands to be with at weekends and holidays.'

There is an added burden to bear because in spite of the increasingly high rate of divorce, it still carries a social stigma. A divorced person very often suffers complete loss of confidence, and a sense of guilt and failure. Other people still consider that a divorced woman constitutes a threat to the marriages of colleagues and friends, so invitations out may be curtailed.

Dr Boon, a consultant psychiatrist in charge of a stress and anxiety unit at a teaching hospital, sees the casualties of divorce and comments, 'Perhaps we should make marriage harder, or at least start educating people about it rather more.' He pinpoints marital breakdown as the second highest cause of stress, more stressful than unemployment or imprisonment. Only the death of husband or wife causes greater stress. Divorce, he has found, can lead to mental breakdown in people who are in no way prone to such illness.

Dr Boon also finds that men are in a worse state than women by the time they see a psychiatrist, probably because they tend to go on longer before seeking help. They often keep the fact of their divorce secret from colleagues or even the family doctor. When a man does tell his friends, they often congratulate him on being one of the boys again and assume that he will relish his regained freedom. A woman's pain is more likely to be recognized and she may receive more support, especially if she has children to care for.

Both men and women who have lost a partner through divorce need to mourn their loss but may not be able to do so in the way that a widow or widower can. The loss is as real and as permanent, and the continuing existence of the one-time partner brings constant reminders of the past. Much that follows, about loss and the way forward for widows and widowers, applies equally to people whose marriage ends in divorce.

C.S. Lewis expressed what Christians generally feel, when he compared divorce to drastic major surgery, only to be resorted to as a last, life-saving act. The pain and distress it causes to everyone involved, and especially to children of the marriage, makes it something to be avoided at all costs except in extreme situations. But Christians should not only uphold the permanence and sanctity of marriage and family life, they should also be the first — as they often are — to give help and support to the victims of marriage breakdown.

Many couples decide to stay together while the children are growing up, then part company by mutual consent when that obligation is over. About one-fifth of all divorces occur between couples who have been married for twenty years or more. The causes may be unfaithfulness, alcoholism, gambling, or just plain dissatisfaction and boredom. It may be a direct consequence of the midlife urge to take off in a different direction, seeking a new way of life and a new partner.

If the children have not yet left home, one partner — often the wife — is left to bring them up single-handed.

One woman talked about the difficulty of coping with a sixteen-year-old son who was six feet tall. 'There's nothing I can do to make him obey,' she said, 'he is dirty and untidy and ruins the expensive clothes I buy for him. When I finally refused to mend one particular pair of trousers, he merely wore them torn.'

Another mother, without her husband for ten years, has three daughters, now aged eighteen, twenty and twenty-two. All want her to listen to them after her day out at work, however late they arrive home. She recognizes their need of a father but wisely realizes that she cannot fulfil both roles. 'I have just tried to be the best possible mother I can to them.'

Recently her husband has told her that he is getting married again. She had known he had a girl friend but, even after ten years, the finality which that spelt for their relationship renewed her pain. His wish to have his daughters at the wedding caused more conflict — two agreeing to go and one refusing. She described the repeated episodes of distress and pain that follow divorce. 'Just as you think the whole thing is over, something happens to open up old wounds again.'

Opportunity for growth

The most painful and the least promising human situations also, amazingly, contain the seeds of something good. In some situations, divorce can be a means of personal growth. Some men and women go straight from divorce into another marriage, imagining that everything will be different this time, only to repeat the mistakes they made the first time. Others wisely use the period following marriage breakdown to sort out their own feelings and to try to discover more about themselves and the ways in which they contributed to the failure of the marriage.

One woman explained what had happened to her: 'All the time in my first marriage I was trying to be the kind of woman he wanted me to be. Suddenly, when the marriage ended, I was free to be myself, the sort of person I really am, without pretending. I could let that self come alive, so that when I married again I was chosen for the person I actually am, and not the image I had presented as a young and immature girl.'

Another woman commented, 'In one way it was the best thing that could have happened to me. In a good marriage a wife can be herself. But not every husband feels strong enough in himself to let his wife develop as a person in her own right. Af first, when my husband began to go away, my self-esteem was pretty low. When he finally left I had a sense of release and I gained confidence in areas I had never known were possible. I had been very young when I first got married and I'd gone straight from my parents' home to my marriage, never having made decisions of my own. It took me five years to find myself and become my own person and the church helped and supported me. Now I'm happy with a husband who allows me to be strong and make decisions too.'

Death

Whenever death comes it shocks. News of it travels like wildfire, as if everyone who hears tries to come to terms with the reality and finality of death by sharing the fact with others. To those who are closest, death is a shock, even after a long illness, when it has been expected and accepted mentally. Naturally the degree of shock is even greater when a person dies following an accident or suddenly, with no history of illness.

One woman, whose story is told in *Drawing Near to the City*, described her sensations as ambulance men tried in vain to revive her husband who had died suddenly in their own living-room: 'I thought, "This is funny. This isn't happening to me — no, it just isn't true." I couldn't believe it. I kept on saying, "No, I can't believe it." But it suddenly dawned on me that really and truly Frank was dead.'

Next morning she and her daughter began to plan what they must do. 'We started the day in a reasonably normal way for ourselves, but it didn't really work. No way was anything going to be normal for me again. . . Halfway through the morning I said, "Oh gosh, is it only half past eleven?" It seemed as if we had been up for ever.'

Another wife, whose husband collapsed and died in a similar way, relived the events over and over, wondering if she had done everything she could to help. She was a practised Red Cross instructor and had used her skills to try to save him. In spite of the doctor's assurances, she still blamed herself.

C.S. Lewis, analysing and recording his own reactions to his wife's death in *A Grief Observed*, described the physical feelings that accompany bereavement. He begins his book, 'No one had ever told me that grief is so like fear. I am not afraid, but the sensation is like being afraid. The same fluttering in the stomach, the same restlessness, the yawning. I keep swallowing.'

But the immediate effect of shock is to bring down a curtain and protect the sufferer from the full impact of what has happened. Immediate decisions and practical plans for the funeral are made without grief having full impact. A bereaved person is not fully conscious of the pain and loss until the first few days are over and the initial shock has worn off.

The various ingredients and stages of grief have been researched and written about, but no two people are likely to react in the same way. Different people progress through the phases of grief at very different rates. Jewish communities set a time for the process, marking out different stages in a year's mourning. Some say that this does not help, as grief does not necessarily fall into neat time slots, but at least those on the outside are provided with clues indicating how to relate to the person who is bereaved.

In Victorian times there was a similar charting of bereavement. The move from one stage to the next was marked by minor changes in dress — from all black to the relief of grey, then lavender and so on. Today there is no way in which the bereavement experience is mapped out and there is no protocol for mourners or sympathizers to follow. Even the homelier church funeral is often replaced by a more impersonal crematorium service, where time is limited and the next cortège is waiting its turn.

Because death is generally a taboo subject and few people have certainties about life after death, no one knows the right words to say to the bereaved person. Many people are so ill at ease in the company of death that, if possible, they avoid contact with the widow or widower altogether. The widow of Keith Blakelock, a policeman brutally killed on duty, spoke about her own experience of friends and neighbours avoiding her because they didn't know what to say. She was touched and comforted when one woman came up to her at church and said, 'I just don't know what to say to you, but I'm so sorry and I want to tell you that.' When people opt out and say nothing, those who are bereaved miss the warmth and comfort they could receive and lose a chance to find release by talking about the one who has died and letting their grief show naturally.

Losing a husband or wife in midlife involves the added sadness of being left alone before the appropriate time. Some feel angry as well as sad, and their anger may even be turned against the partner who has died. They feel cheated of the years together that they had expected to enjoy. As a couple they have been through shared years of hard work, money worries, family cares and pressure at work as well as at home. They had reached an age where the end of these difficulties was in view and the prospect of a happy new chapter in their marriage lay ahead of them. That future has been taken away and all that lies in store seems to be pain, difficulty and loss. Since women normally live longer than men, a widower may feel the unfairness of the loss even more keenly. But a man is more likely to remarry, since there are far fewer widowers than widows in their forties and fifties.

In the early days after the husband's death many widows panic about money. They are often uncertain how they stand financially. If the husband has always paid the bills and seen to the business side of things, a widow may feel utterly confused and extremely anxious and burdened. Unless she is already earning enough to support herself and any of the family still at school or in training, as well as keep the house going, she is likely to have to go through a time of uncertainty. Legal and tax wheels grind slowly and it can be up to nine months before probate is given. If the husband has not made a will, things will be far more complicated. Some couples wrongly assume that everything will go automatically to the partner on their death and therefore a will is unnecessary. Others, because they are superstitious or just never get round to it, don't make a will either.

People who would not dream of being slack about taking out full insurance, still die intestate — and the number includes bank managers and others whose daily job should make them only too aware of the problems that can arise. It is important to make sure that a will is kept up to date, amending it when there is a change in address or when children are adult. It is necessary to make a new will when there is a change of name. These days, when remarriage of partners and their children complicates family affairs further, making a will is even more essential.

Most new widows worry about responsibility for the house. Usually the property will be in joint names. Now she is solely responsible. She has never owned anything so valuable before and may begin to worry about any major repairs that will be needed and even be afraid that the roof may blow off. Some widows rush to make economies before they know what their financial situation really is and move into a smaller house before they are ready to make such a big decision. Later they find that the economy was not necessary. It is far wiser to sit tight until the true financial situation is known and until things have straightened out enough for wise decisions to be taken. Often there is a family friend with some financial expertise to give immediate help, or the late husband's employers may advise on business affairs.

Sometimes the motive for the move is to be nearer a son or daughter. It is sometimes the case that in going to be near them they also choose to move into a new and older age bracket while they are still relatively young. This happens if they become dependent on their son or daughter. It might be better to consider sheltered accommodation, where there is freedom and independence, with the built-in guarantee of future care.

There are organizations — CRUSE in the UK, for example — that have been set up to give widows and widowers, and their families, counsel and support, often at local as well as national level.

Loss

Some widows feel a loss of identity when their husband dies. Although some wives have their own career and their own colleagues and friends, others who have reached midlife have not worked outside the home. For the past ten or twenty years they have taken their identity from husband and children. They are someone's wife and somebody's mother. If the children are also leaving home at the time when the husband dies, a woman's identity and even her reasons for living may be withdrawn at the same time. Her status in life has also depended on her husband's position in the community. Being a widow, even of someone who was of consequence, soon loses its potency and when her grief and pain are most acute a woman may also have to cope with the sense of being nothing and nobody in her own right. Some continue to mourn and cling to the old times long after the usual period of intense grieving is past, because they are unable to find an identity of their own and can only live again, in memory, the times when they believe that they counted for something.

Some women widowed in midlife also feel that they have lost their femininity. The menopause coupled with a sense of having lost youthful good looks and sex appeal may already have made them unsure of their attractiveness as women. The husband's death not only denies them sexual expression but also signifies the loss of the one person who found them feminine, desirable and supremely important. The companion with whom they could talk, discuss and laugh about life has also gone. Fun and laughter are important ingredients of marriage and a valuable part of everyday living, putting perspective as well as sparkle into the big and small matters of life. But not many friends will think it seemly to share a joke or a good laugh with a widow for some time to come.

Up to now, the assumption has been that the marriage was a good one. It might be imagined that grieving and mourning are most intense when the relationship has been good. In fact the opposite seems true. Those who have had an unsatisfactory marriage seem to find the mourning process even more difficult. If a poor marriage has survived until midlife, it is likely to have accumulated a great many resentments and some bitterness. The grieving that follows the death of one partner will also include mourning for what the relationship might have been and even how it was at the beginning of the marriage. Those who have had stormy marriages actually seem to miss the exhilaration of the rows!

A childless widow may mourn her childlessness, probably now final, and the children that she and her husband never had, or the baby they lost. She will feel different from other widows who are surrounded by their family. She may also find herself less well off financially than they are.

A widow with children may find them a great comfort, especially if the family can share their grief together. Sometimes children who are going through the difficult stage of adolescence, or facing crises of their own, may turn in anger on their mother, even showing physical violence towards her. They may resent the fact that she has taken on the authority and decision-making of the lost father.

The way forward

There are two main ingredients in the experience of bereavement at any age but especially so in the case of a husband or wife left alone in midlife.

First, there is the need to mourn and work through the grief. This stage is a little like that of convalescence after illness, except that someone who has been ill can return virtually unchanged to full health, while a bereaved person is never going to be quite the same as before. However well a widow or widower may appear to 'get over it', as people say, they will not be the same person again. They may end up more independent and more fulfilled and happy, but they will be different. Some say that the first year of bereavement is the worst, bringing the initial round of special anniversaries to be faced alone. Others would claim that a year is far too short a time in which to recover 'normal' feelings and reactions to life.

People vary in the time it takes them to come to terms with their grief and work through the period of intense sadness and mourning for the dead. What is certain is that no one can afford to bypass or even short-cut the process of grieving. Those who try to deny grief its full impact and fill their lives with activity and new involvements almost at once, often face a time of mourning later. It may be triggered by the death of someone far less close, or even by the loss of a pet animal. The unreleased grief of the earlier, major bereavement eventually finds a way out.

The second ingredient of bereavement is the search for a way forward. Some widowed people try to reach this stage too soon. They arrange a round of activity which will prevent the silence and solitude that might leave room for pain and tears. Others feel unable to plan a positive future alone. They may feel guilty at the thought of grieving less as months or years pass. But, important as the grieving time is, the need to find a new pattern of life is essential.

Most widowers and some widows have no choice but to return to work after a very short absence. A widow may have to set about an instant change in lifestyle in order to survive and support the family. But there are widows and widowers who seem to make no attempt to return to normality and do not progress beyond their grief. They remain in a kind of time warp, unable or unwilling to begin to plan a new pattern of living. It is important to discover when the time is right to begin thinking of the future, and to plan positively. Courage and honesty are needed, both to resist pressure from others to speed up the process, and to react positively when the time has come to adapt and make changes for the future.

Join something!

In their attempts to help a widow, friends may encourage her to join something. But it is not always easy for a man or woman in their forties or fifties to know what to join. Too often, widows find themselves mixing with one another and that is not always what is needed. Many women who have no ulterior motives feel the lack of men's company and the stimulus of mixed discussions.

One widow told me of her own experiences. Friends at church frequently invited her to Sunday lunch, but almost always she found that they had invited three or four other widows too. 'Being with other widows is the last thing I feel like,' she said, 'they all want to talk about how their husbands died. What I am pining for is the stimulus of a bit of male conversation.' It is easy for those of us who have not been through the experience to offer the wrong kind of help. We must use our imagination and listen to what people tell us if we are to give the help that is needed.

Some widows and widowers try to lay the ghost of past memories by moving house. The bungalow by the sea or in the country may seem the ideal way to banish painful memories, and the excitement of the move and the new surroundings often do bring a temporary boost to morale. But a change of house does not change the person who has moved there, and the added loneliness of leaving friends and familiar surroundings may make their unhappiness greater.

Others try to find comfort by marrying again. When a person marries for the relief and solace a new partner can bring, rather than for the person themselves, the new relationship may not be founded firmly enough to endure. A husband or wife who perfectly fills the role of comforter may not be a suitable partner once the initial period of mourning is past. Remarriage only works when both partners come to it with personalities recovered sufficiently to give as well as take. The relationship must be sound in its own right, not entered into as an attempt to recapture what has gone or to provide consolation.

Some widows are tempted to take on the role of child to

their own grown-up children, depending on them for practical and emotional needs, but this kind of relationship will restrict everyone involved and prevent the bereaved person from continuing to grow and develop as a human being.

'At first, my daughter would ring me up every night before bedtime,' one widow confessed, 'but after the first difficult weeks I realized that I must break the habit before it became too demanding for her as well as stopping me from learning to be independent.'

Preparing for loss

Although it can be morbid to think too much beforehand about a partner's death, it is reasonable and right to make certain preparations in case one or other should die early. Both partners should make a will and keep it up-to-date. One partner may handle the money side of the marriage, but it is important that the other knows what the money situation is. Both should know where any relevant documents are kept and how to cope with banks, building societies and insurance companies. It is helpful when both can drive the car. Some women have the pluck to learn to drive soon after their husband's death, but it is far better to learn at a time when there is no additional emotional stress. Men who have never had to cook a meal, use the washing-machine or go shopping, should be taught the bare essentials of coping with household jobs. Women would feel less at a loss if they learned simple maintenance, such as mending a fuse, changing a plug or washer, or checking car tyres. (I haven't yet done anything about that myself.)

Faith

Some people say that they lost their faith in God when they were bereaved. Perhaps it would be truer to say that before this their faith had not been seriously thought out, or had never before been put to the test. When someone assumes that faith in God guarantees protection from the nastier experiences of life, they are in for a rude awakening. God does not promise to keep us free from disaster or suffering, but to be with us in it and to bring something good out of it.

Even those whose faith in God has been solidly based may find that faith apparently shattered when death takes away the person they love most. In *A Grief Observed*, C.S. Lewis recorded his feelings on the death of his wife. His initial reaction was, 'Meanwhile, where is God?' But not very long after, he discovered that 'turned to God I no longer meet a locked door'.

Many widows and widowers can vouch for an amazing sense of God's closeness and peace during the very worst moments of loss, whereas others hold on to the *knowledge* of God's presence in spite of their feeling of desolation. They also draw strength from the loving closeness of friends and from those who pray for them. In the end, theological explanation of the question 'Why?' matters less than the reassurance and comfort of another human being who is prepared to come alongside, to listen, to refrain from platitudes and offer the warmth and comfort of their presence. God cannot be less loving and caring than one of his children.

Amazingly, loss and pain in bereavement, and in every other area of life, can also be a medium for growth and transformation. A man or woman who has suffered, and has finally accepted loss without bitterness or self-pity, is immeasurably more compassionate, more fully human and more able to help others.

ACTION CHECKPOINTS

☐ Capitalize on the benefits of being alone.

☐ Look for ways of being alone and not lonely.

☐ Use imagination in trying to help those bereaved by death or divorce.

☐ Give grief time.

☐ Be ready to move forward when the right time comes.

☐ Make practical preparations for being independent — house–hold skills, etc.

☐ Make a will — make a new will when necessary.

SECTION 6
THE WORLD OF WORK

15
WORKING LIFE

The Things People Say

'I feel it's hardly right getting paid for the job, because I so enjoy what I'm doing!'
BBC cameraman

'The first three days of holiday he talks about nothing but work. He just can't unwind.'
Wife of middle manager

'Don't feel sorry for me. I really like what I do.'
Matron of old people's nursing home

'Well, it's a job, isn't it? That's what matters for the moment and it could be a lot worse. I don't hate it.'
Salesman

'By Thursday I'd worked the requisite number of hours for the whole week. But I shan't take time off, there's too much to do. And it's worthwhile, in spite of the disappointments and the strain.'
Prison probation officer

'Being a general surgeon is really very boring after a few years.'
Middle-aged surgeon

'The Bible makes clear that human work is to reflect God's work. . . The human race is to live on the earth and master its laws. This was the original meaning of work. It is a far cry from today's popular view that work equals a job.'
Michael Moynagh, *Making Unemployment Work*

One of the commonest ways of starting up conversation with a fellow guest at a party is to ask, 'What do you do?' It's a useful opening gambit because it tells us something about the stranger, as well as leading on naturally to further talk. But the reason why we ask the question may go deeper than social custom and usefulness.

In our society a person is judged to some extent at least by the job they do. Many of us assume, falsely, that 'I am what I do'. The unemployed feel losers right away, because they can give no identifying answer to the polite questioner. Many women answer, 'I'm just a housewife,' betraying their acceptance of motherhood and house care as second-rate occupations. Among those who are employed there is general recognition that society applies its own scale, often unrelated to the real value of the job. There is more prestige, for example, in being a television presenter than a sewerage worker, although the latter is probably of greater value to the community. Status, in turn, is often linked with salary. Most of the caring professions, with the exception of medicine but including education, are low paid and low rated in consequence. At midlife we need to think realistically about the true value of the work we do, rather than accept society's flawed standards.

There is a good deal of talk these days about basic human rights and many of us would agree that the right to work is one of them. But, of course, a lot depends on what we call work. One sociologist believes that work involves:

- expending energy

- providing goods or a service

- providing social status for the worker

- defining the way in which we relate socially

Bringing in money

The definition of work as a means of bringing in money, like most others, fails to fit the bill completely. As another writer points out, it gives a chef preparing a meal the dignity of doing a job but fails to include a housewife who is cooking the dinner, since she is not receiving pay. Others define work as what we don't like doing, whereas leisure activity is what we enjoy. But there are plenty of people lucky enough to enjoy the job they are paid to do.

Most of us can see that however we may have defined work in the past we are going to have to think again and revise our notions in order to adapt more realistically to present and future patterns of life in the West. What matters more, we must change our attitudes to work if we are to give everyone in society a sense of worth and the opportunity to be of value in the community.

Midlife shake-up

Midlife is the time when most people have to stop and take stock in the world of work as well as in other areas of life. Even if no outward changes are made, it is still important for us to weigh up the successes and failures as well as the degree of satisfaction the job brings. It may also be necessary to bring out into the open some of the fears and frustrations that can be undermining our peace of mind.

Success story

Some men and women at midlife have actually achieved their ambitions at work, whether in the professions or in industry. Others set out to get rich and make their million by the time they are forty — or younger. To the rest of us, such people are obvious successes but, surprisingly, the people themselves may be deeply dissatisfied. The glamour attached to some jobs is mostly in the eye of the beholder.

In fact, many people who have succeeded in their job, or who hold enviable positions and corresponding salaries, are frustrated and unhappy in midlife. Once an ambition has been realized, the earlier excitement and satisfaction of working towards a goal is over.

The successful person suffers from what has been called the Alexander syndrome — the despair of knowing that there are no more worlds left to conquer. Working towards achievement can be deeply fulfilling. Once the target is reached, life can seem pointless and empty.

The best-selling author, Frederick Forsyth, interviewed some years ago, talked about his career in this way. 'If I were interviewing myself I would say, "You wanted to become a pilot, you became one. You wanted to be a reporter, you became one. You wanted to be a foreign correspondent, you became one. You wanted to make money, you made it. Where then was the failure?" — Because there was failure.' Those who have been outwardly successful need to ask the same question and to discern ways of achieving other kinds of success.

In work, as in other areas of life, men and women in their forties and fifties may need to set new goals which will satisfy them for the second half of life. The successful person may not necessarily aim even higher than before in their particular field, but may see the need for a change of direction. Achievement in any area requires single-mindedness and intense application. Many who have reached the top by midlife may become aware that, although part of them has been stretched to the utmost, other gifts and personality traits have been left fallow.

Some may feel that one side of their nature has been developed to the detriment of the other. Many have succeeded at the expense of the gentler side of their nature. Some men may find, too late, that they have had no time to get to know their own children. Now they long to show love and friendship to children who have grown up accustomed to managing without a father's attention and affection. Other men may realize that they have been too busy to nurture their marriage and give tenderness and time to their wife.

Most people won't have given a thought to the spiritual side of their nature, or to the achieving of spiritual goals, which include finding out about God and answering some of the big questions about the meaning of life and what lies beyond it. If issues like this, the ones that really matter, have been shelved since teenage days, midlife is the time to look at them again. It is time to examine some of the answers with an open mind. It is worth reading the Bible — especially the New Testament Gospels — in a modern translation, with an open mind and with adult understanding and experience. Look at people who have put that lifestyle into practice, to some extent at least. I once heard someone describe her experience when, as a child, she was first fitted with a pair of spectacles. She saw things that she had never known existed and the world became a richer and fuller place. Looking at the world through God's eyes, in the light of what Jesus said and did, can transform life even more dramatically. We can come into a whole new appreciation of all that life is meant to be. Jesus told his followers, 'I have come in order that you might have life — life in all its fulness.'

Sold short

Those who have achieved the goals they set for themselves in their chosen career are probably far fewer in number than those who reach midlife realizing not only that their goals have not been reached but that they are now highly unlikely to make the grade. To themselves they are failures. Athletes and sports people know for sure when they have reached the age at which it is too late to compete and win. What is true in the boxing ring or on the football field, applies in other areas too. People in industry or academia know that if they have not reached a particular rung on the ladder by the time they are a certain age, they have little hope of getting to the top before retirement.

Some may feel bitter, believing that they had the potential for promotion but were passed over or ruthlessly kicked to the bottom by more aggressive colleagues. Somehow they must come to terms with their frustration, if they are not to be damaged by destructive emotions for the rest of their life. How they do so is another matter. One man I know had his career as well as his future pension rights harmed by a particularly vindictive boss. It took him several years to recognize that he needed to deal with his own desire to get even with the man who had injured him. He had to face his own need to forgive as well as to put his whole work situation into God's hands and let him deal with it. Those who are willing to turn to God for help in this kind of situation discover that he is able to give the motive and the grace to forgive and also to bring something positive and good out of the setbacks and limitations imposed by others.

Another group of workers find themselves stuck in jobs which fail to satisfy their needs and abilities. Some are doing boring repetitive jobs which have little human interest. At forty, the realization comes that another twenty or more years of such work lies ahead. At least the job may leave spare mental and creative energy which can be used in out-of-work time. But it would be useless to pretend that there are wholly satisfying solutions to this or the other work crises of midlife. While some will take refuge in getting through work as a means to an end — collecting the pay packet and enjoying home life, hobbies and holidays — others may find the resources to turn even an uninteresting job into a means of self-expression, giving stature to a job that lacks human interest or dignity by doing it reliably, with integrity and with consideration for the other human beings involved.

Meeting the demands

Most jobs these days are extremely demanding and this may be especially true for men and women in their forties. The slimming down of work forces in recent years means that everyone still in work is stretched to the limit. There is no longer any slack to be taken up in the system. The increased use of machines to do routine work saves time but also means that the relaxation of doing non-demanding tasks has been largely eliminated. That sounds fine in theory but it increases the intensity of the job and speeds up the rate at which decision-making and the more taxing aspects of work must be carried out. Better communication systems mean that a person is never out of reach of his or her firm, and jetting around the world for sales deals and conferences adds to the pressure.

Further stress is caused by the fact that both small and large firms work on slim profit margins, so that right decisions become increasingly important. Those employed in medicine and education as well as industry and business face difficult decision-making in the light of cuts and economies. The self-employed have pressures too. Success often depends on working flat out. It's difficult to take time off, and their work load is increased by form-filling, and all the paper work which has become a part of our way of life.

Of course, there are the corresponding satisfactions. Many people find their job intensely interesting. They know that they are needed and that their decisions are helping to meet human need or make the business efficient and profitable. One man in his fifties, working for a large food firm, said, 'I love my work — I really enjoy it. But the other day I went in at eight o'clock in the morning and left at six in the evening with more problems remaining than I had solved. By mid-afternoon I felt pretty desperate. So I pulled my Bible out of the drawer in the desk where I keep it. I read a few verses and quietly prayed. It gave me the peace and the strength to go on.' Sadly, more people react like the senior manager who commented, 'After the kind of stresses I have at work I need two double whiskies straight off by the time I get home.'

Another pressure for many people in midlife is the need to keep abreast of new skills and new areas of knowledge in their particular trade or profession. Some employees may be sent on courses and required to make use of new techniques or devices. Others need to read an increasing number of journals in order to keep abreast of research in their field. In midlife many have difficulty in finding time and enthusiasm to acquire or adapt to so much that is new. There is sometimes the fear that younger colleagues may be more closely in touch with new methods, and faster at picking up the required knowledge and expertise. Again, it is important to come to terms with the situation and to recognize and accept the cost of keeping among the front runners, or be prepared to fall back, when that is possible, and enjoy other kinds of achievement and success.

There are other fears in midlife for those at work. Business takeovers are common and when these occur some staff usually become redundant. One middle management employee said,

'There are rumours that our firm could be taken over. There are 547 people employed where I am and the other firm has said that if they take us over they will keep only forty of our staff. I don't see why I should think that I'll be one of the forty.'

Larger units also involve fewer at the top, limiting promotion. Financial cuts also make chances of promotion rarer.

After such a list of problems and constraints it might be easy to conclude that everyone in their forties or fifties is unhappy or under intolerable pressure at work. Of course that isn't so. But it is reassuring to realize that it is perfectly normal to feel under pressure, and that it is important to pause long enough to take a look at your own situation. Try to pinpoint any stress and look for solutions. It may not be possible to change things at work, but you may be able to cut down extra strains, or create more time for exercise and relaxation outside work.

It is important that couples understand each other's needs. A wife who is coping with the menopause, looking after parents and meeting the demands of teenage children, may not be aware of the fact that her husband has problems and needs of his own. When one partner is over-working, there is always a knock-on effect on the other. So any plans for easing up need to be thought out and planned together.

Double work load

Many of the men coping with problems at work will not have a wife waiting at home to dish out hot dinner and sympathy when they get back at night. Plenty of women who run a home and look after children prefer to work at a job outside the home as well. They may do so for a variety of reasons.

Some have never contemplated doing anything else. They took time off to have their babies, returning as soon as possible.

Others took a break of ten years or so, until all the children started school, then went back to their job. These women probably work outside the home because they believe that they are trained and suited to their job and can only find full satisfaction by continuing to do it.

There are others who go out to work in order to earn money. Sometimes their reason is only too valid. Single mothers in particular may find it necessary but there are also plenty of two-parent families where both incomes are needed to keep the home going. But opinions vary as to where necessity ends and luxury begins. Some mothers go out to work because they don't want their children to go without what everyone else seems to have. Children learn from advertising what is on offer and compare what they have with what their friends at school possess. Many parents are genuinely afraid that their children will suffer seriously if they don't have designer jeans or the latest electronic device. It is worth thinking and talking through this particular issue with the children themselves as soon as they are old enough to understand. If they know that the choice is between having more things and having their parent at home, some may actually prefer more time and attention from the parent rather than the things which extra earnings can buy. Children and teenagers need to be helped to get their priorities right, but it can be difficult for all the family to sort out what matters most in our affluent and materialist society.

Sometimes unconscious pressure is put on a married woman to return to her profession. Everyone just takes it for granted that no mother is likely to remain at home if she has a good job to return to.

'Of course you will go back to your midwifery now,' neighbours kept saying to Jan when her youngest and last child was due to start school. Jan admitted that she was strongly tempted to do so. The low status of child-caring means that she would easily be able to afford the cost of someone to look after her children at times when they were at home and she was on duty. But she resisted the pressure. She considered that her children would benefit more from having her around when they came home from school, during the holidays, or when they were ill. She also thought of the many other people who ring her up when they are depressed, come to drink coffee and pour out their troubles and generally make her their confidante and helper at church and in her home. She decided to remain a full-time wife and mother for a few more years.

Others would like to resist pressure to return to an outside job — and sometimes do — because they happen to prefer running a home and bringing up a family. Women's liberation, rightly interpreted, should surely mean freedom to choose — and freedom for those women who enjoy being at home to remain there, provided there is sufficient money to support the family.

Mixed blessings

A recent survey revealed that in spite of the help that most husbands now give in the home, it still falls to the wife, in almost every case, to be responsible for household and child management. It is she who is the brains behind the operation.

As one woman put it, 'He's awfully good about shopping, but I'm the one who has to make out the list and master-mind the meal planning.' Fathers often spend time playing with their children and keeping them amused, but mothers usually prepare their meals or change the nappies. Those now in their forties and fifties are likely to be less, rather than more, enlightened in sharing housework. So most women who choose to work outside the home are still responsible for most of the organizing of home and family.

Many women pay the price for doing a double job in terms of chronic fatigue. In her book, *Women and Fatigue*, American medical journalist Dr Holly Atkinson pinpoints constant, nagging tiredness as the female epidemic of the eighties, and attributes it to 'having it all'. She suggests that if women wish to work outside the home as well as in it, they must take a long look at their lifestyle and decide what can go, to enable them to survive. Her advice is to jettison over-high standards of cleanliness in the house. 'The problem,' she comments, 'is that having a pristine home is inexplicably linked to a woman's ability as a wife and homemaker. It's part of her identity. That should change.'

It is certainly worthwhile to review the multitude of jobs that fill the day and week and decide what cuts can be made, especially during the menopause, in order to have enough energy to do what has to be done and to enjoy personal relationships as well as to enjoy life.

Guilt as well as tiredness may plague the working wife and mother. Although she may feel she is right to return to work, she may still be anxious that she is short-changing either her job or her family or both. In theory it is easier to work when children are older but in practice mothers may discover that children in their early teens have needs just as pressing as when they were young, but less easily met by a paid helper. Even when a mother has a clear conscience she may feel pulled in two directions, with the conflicting claims of home and work. Some women find excellent help at home and organize their time without due strain, but families as well as helps can be unpredictable.

Women tend to be employed in the caring professions, such as teaching, medicine and social work. These jobs make heavy emotional demands as well as calling for a flexible approach to time on duty. I understood the dilemma of the doctor who told me that she could not spare long for my appointment as she had a waiting-room full and had to finish surgery in order to take her daughter for a check-up. But I still expected her to give her patients her full time and attention while she was at work.

The unmarried matron of a nursing home for elderly people told me that she finds it hard to get dedicated staff. Her comment was: 'These days they are all married and they phone up to say they can't come on duty because their husband is off work, or ask for leave because a daughter is having a baby. Even when they are at work they are watching the clock.'

Most people could make some changes, however small, to relieve the tiredness and work load. Some possibilities are:

• cut down on working hours

• ask for leave of absence — until menopause or other stressful period is over

• get help — with ironing, cleaning, gardening

• buy time-saving, labour-saving devices

• set lower standards in house-cleaning, entertaining etc. — at least as a temporary measure

• set time aside — however short — for relaxation, formal or informal.

Midlife should be a time for coming to terms with life as it really is, even when that means seeming to achieve less for a time. Relieving the pressure for a short while by some means or other may avoid illness or depression and help others in the family who are also under stress.

Housework

The vast majority of women between the ages of sixteen and sixty-five are housewives. 'Housewife' is a term used to define the person responsible for most household duties and includes both married and single, whether or not they are employed outside the home.

Many women in their forties and fifties have no outside job and they may feel their hackles rise when they are asked, 'Do you work?', meaning, 'Do you have a paid job outside the home?' Fifteen years or more ago a sociologist commented, 'Women today are considered to have two choices — to work or to stay at home. This implies that staying at home does not involve work.' Perhaps it is because housework does not fit the definition of work as something for which a person is paid, that it is discounted in such a way. But it is a sad reflection on the value placed on child-rearing and home-making that house-work is given such low status.

In the fifties, Betty Friedan stated that 'housework expands to fill the time available' and, although in the early years of having a family it is probably true that a woman's work is never done, there should not be the same pressure in midlife, unless there are special circumstances. Sadly, many women feel impelled to justify their existence, and to disprove those who imply that there isn't much to running a home, by setting increasingly high standards for themselves. The fact that they have to structure their own working day and set their own standards often impels them to follow a far harder regime than an employer would expect.

Coralie, whose two children are in their teens, insists on moving every piece of furniture and cleaning thoroughly every week, even though there is very little dirt and dust to matter. She told me that she looked forward to the time when she would be free to go out and about after her family had left home. But she will find it hard to break free from her self-imposed routine. Because there is no clocking-off time, many housewives never take time off or devise any ways of relieving the boredom or routine of the day.

Men sometimes ask in amazement why a woman should look for a job outside the home when she could be so much more free as a housewife. They probably point out too that the paid jobs they take are not half as interesting as cooking or caring for a family. The answer is partly that an outside job brings status, a wage packet, and a bit of independence, but also that a job provides social contacts. Housework is one of the few jobs done in isolation. In almost every other job, people at work are mixing together. A housewife may stop for a few minutes to chat to a neighbour, but her work is done alone. Perhaps there are areas where this isolation could be overcome. A group of women could share out the jobs — taking it in turns to do ironing or baking for each other, or teaming up to tackle the gardening.

Women who are 'only housewives' are in danger of suffer-ing from stress just as much as their husbands. It is important that they should recognize the danger of driving themselves to unnecessarily high standards and of undervaluing their work. They also need to combat the loneliness and monotony of some household jobs by deliberately finding social outlets and begin-ning to form links with the outside world, where they may soon be freer and readier to return in voluntary or paid employment, for part at least of their working week.

ACTION CHECKPOINTS

☐ Rethink work goals.

☐ Look for ways to relieve pressure at work.

☐ Look for practical ways of relieving chronic fatigue.

☐ Sort out priorities and make work choices accordingly.

☐ Cut down on unnecessary housework and find ways of making it less lonely.

NEW WORK — NEW LEISURE

The Things People Say

'However much you may have been prepared for it beforehand, when the time comes "early retirement", as they politely call it, is always a shock.'
Middle manager, 'retired' in his fifties

'Many Christians today believe that the Protestant work ethic, as it has come to be understood, is a fundamental misinterpretation of what the Bible says about work and its relation to personal value.'
Michael Moynagh, *Making Unemployment Work*

'When you meet them, avoid continually asking them whether there are any jobs coming up.'
How to Help the Jobless, Salvation Army

'I love my half day helping in the charity shop. I meet so many people and those of us who help get together too.'
Voluntary helper

'Most people feel that they should look busy, because busyness is equated with being of value. It takes courage to admit, "I haven't got anything in my diary"!'

'It's important to have time to be available for other people — there aren't too many who are.'

'In about twenty-five years' time it will take no more than ten per cent of the labour force to supply society with all its material needs.'
Prof. Tom Storrie, quoted by Ann Warren, in *Living with Unemployment*

'I do miss dressing to look smart now that I've stopped going out to work. There's nothing to dress up for at home.'

When we look ahead, we can envisage the time when most people will finish working long before the present retirement age. Meanwhile most of us find it hard to be 'put out to grass' before that stage. But, as we have already said, many people in midlife face redundancy or enforced early retirement as the result of takeovers, government cuts or slimming down of work forces because of greater automation.

It is easy to enjoy the idea of early retirement in theory, and some who choose to go thoroughly enjoy the freedom. For many others, the effects can be particularly devastating. Loss of income usually coincides with the time when most people are financially committed up to the hilt. Almost more important, the trauma of unemployment adds to the sum of midlife self-doubt and insecurity.

Sometimes the brutal way in which the matter is handled adds to the trauma. One man was told on a Friday that his job was to finish that day. A colleague of his was told one evening not to come in again. Because he could not carry his accumulated belongings back that evening, the two men returned early the next morning, before work, to collect what remained from his locker, only to find that the locks had already been changed.

Even when due warning is given and the whole matter is dealt with sensitively, the person made redundant is likely to suffer immediate shock followed by a period of loss similar to that of any other bereavement. Most employees feel deeply hurt that their skills and loyalty have counted for nothing and that they have been rejected. Self-confidence takes a hard knock and those who depend on their job for a sense of worth and identity are very badly hit. People are far more than the job they do, but society fails to recognize the fact, so it is not surprising that losing a job in midlife has serious effects. Some firms give a generous golden handshake and an adequate pension but other employees have money worries to add to their problems. Short-term, the outlook can be grim.

Out of work

The effects of unemployment follow a predictable pattern. Michael Moynagh, in *Making Unemployment Work*, calls them steps into despair and defines them as a downward progression of:

- shock

- denial

- search

- despair
- resignation

The initial shock may give rise to physical symptoms. One man talked of feeling as if he had been hit in the stomach. Loss of appetite, loss of sexual drive, lethargy and tiredness are frequent short- or long-term effects. For a while shock blocks out the full implications. As in bereavement, there may be an inability to take in the truth and finality of what has happened. It is only after repeated fruitless attempts to get work that feelings of despair take hold.

Ann Warren, in *Living with Unemployment*, describes the effect on both her and her husband when a Stock Exchange takeover left him without a job. She discovered that people in this situation do not often talk about their deep feelings and needs. Those who have not had the experience may be unaware of the pain and the loss of confidence that an unemployed person is facing. Anger and bitterness may compound the problem.

One woman whose husband lost his job about ten years ago, and who now has part-time work, still speaks with great bitterness and anger about the way in which he was treated. Negative feelings of loss, even betrayal, are common. If they fail in due time to give place to more positive emotions, the people concerned can be permanently damaged and hurt.

At some point a wife, mother or close friend may need to encourage the unemployed person to come to terms with what has happened and try to construct a future, with or without a job. But love, gentleness and wisdom are needed to know the right time and the right way to give such advice.

The way ahead will vary from person to person. In a town where the close-down of an industry puts half the adult population on the dole, it may prove impossible to find a new job. Those who are free to move away, or who live in areas where jobs are more plentiful, may need advice and help to find the right work. In most countries there are government schemes for retraining and often free assessment of a person's skills as well as help in applying for jobs. There are also private firms which charge high fees but give more individual and tailor-made recommendations. They are usually geared to professional people. They draw up CVs and help clients to sell themselves to the prospective employers.

Churches in some high unemployment areas have opened centres where unemployed people can meet and find support from one another and receive help from professional advisers. Others have set up workshops and provided employment opportunities. Those who have lost their jobs need the opportunity to share their feelings of confusion and despair with others in the same boat, or with people who will listen and give support in an understanding way.

Some of those who have experienced redundancy mention ways in which they learned to keep up morale and avoid slipping into the dead-end state that can affect anyone who is out of work for long. They advise:

- Get up promptly and dress properly.

- Don't slop around all day in slippers.

- Get shaved/put on make-up.

- Keep to working hours only, for filling up forms, job applications and so on.

- Take the evenings off as you would when at work.

- Get enough physical activity — gardening, jogging, walking.

- Think in terms of helping others.

When a married man is unemployed his wife often bears the full brunt of his pain and anger. In an area of high unemployment she may also be coping with teenage children who can't get work. She often makes superhuman efforts to keep bright and optimistic in order to support her husband, refusing to share the load with others out of loyalty to him. For his part, he may not only feel rejected at work but an inadequate husband and father. If his wife has been able to get work and is now at a regular job while he remains at home, his confidence may be further sapped.

In a stable marriage where each feels secure in the love and respect of the other, both may be able to withstand the strains but even where relationships are good, much tact and understanding will be needed. When a wife comes to the end of her tether, it may be best for her to let her husband know how she feels, so that he can give her help too and they can return to the normal and healthier habit of each supporting the other. The key is to be open and understanding with each other. It is easy to become self-absorbed or to vent feelings of unhappiness and frustration on the partner. Pooling your feelings and your fears, and together facing the present and the future can bring you close. Some couples come through the crisis with a stronger, better marriage and a greater understanding of each other.

There is a need for those with counselling skills to give professional advice to unemployed people, providing help in practical as well as emotional matters. Some unemployed people might consider setting up a self-help group, where members could provide one another with support. Even more important is the need for those of us who have work to change our attitudes.

In *Issues Facing Christians Today*, the Rev. John Stott writes, 'Many of us need to change our attitudes towards the unemployed and persuade the public to do the same. Those who have been schooled in the values of the so-called "Protestant Work Ethic" (industry, honesty, resourcefulness, thrift, etc.) tend to despise those who are losers in the struggle to survive, as if it were their fault. . . The great majority of unemployed people want to work, but cannot find a job. They are victims of the recession and the new technology. There is need therefore for more Christian sympathy towards them and more pastoral care. We have to repent of looking down on the unemployed, and of ever imagining that the words "workless" and "worthless" might be synonyms.'

Those who honestly believe that status and money are not the most important values in life and that a person's worth is not determined by his job, will be better able to face unemployment in a positive way, although the pain and loss will be just as real. As Michael Moynagh puts it, 'Their humanity, not their work, gives their lives meaning.' He illustrates this with a story: 'It is as if two people were walking in the countryside. There is a rock in the path. To one of the hikers the rock is of no value. He moves to push it away. His friend, who is a sculptor, stops him. "Don't push it away," he says. "It may seem no use to you, but I can see in it a beautiful sculpture." So the sculptor takes the rock, chisels away and turns it into an exquisite masterpiece. God says something similar to. . . all the unemployed who are in despair.'

Illness

Some men and women have to stop work early because of ill-health. For a man it may be his first real experience of staying at home. Only those who stay or work at home know how easy it is to become demoralized by small things — grey skies or the non-arrival of the post. There are advantages. No waiting for trains that don't arrive, or sitting in traffic jams, or braving a walk or cycle ride through rain and snow. But the person who feels cheated of twenty or more years of working life may find it hard to count blessings or to find a purpose for living. Coping with pain or disability in addition can make the daily routine an obstacle course. We need to come to terms with the loss of:

- health and physical abilities

- job satisfaction

- achievement at work

- status of the job

- earned income

- social contacts at work

- future promotion.

One woman, who was forced through ill-health to retire when she was at the top of her professional career, found herself asking: 'Can I really grow, feel worthwhile and go on having something to give without the stimuli and rewards I have been accustomed to? I did trust God's providence but at first it would have been phoney to smile and pretend that there was no pain. I found relief in the end when I realized that God knows me through and through — my weaknesses as well as my strengths. I decided that trying to pack my life full again, in other ways, would only boost my morale. I've had to rethink values in a practical way. I want to leave time, so that I can be available, in a world where everyone is too busy to listen or help.'

The illness of a partner can bring a similar need to rethink and change patterns of work. A wife sometimes has to adapt to a new way of life because the permanent effects of a heart attack or stroke make it impossible for her husband to resume his job or his previous role. Both partners have to adapt, learn new roles and new skills too. The wife may have to go out to work, perhaps for the first time. Or what was a second salary may now become the main source of income. How successfully they both come to terms with the changes will depend partly on how flexible the marriage has been.

One woman of forty plus, whose husband had undergone drastic heart surgery, described how the problems began once he was getting better. She had married young, never having lived apart from her parents, and as a couple they had kept to fairly fixed roles within the marriage. He had always budgeted the money and when she had to deal with the bills he still insisted, from his hospital bed, that she should do it his way. But, for the first time, she was carrying the responsibility for their joint lives.

Looking back, she can see positive gains in their relationship and in their separate development as people since the shake-up. Together they have sorted out some of the important issues of life and decided where their marriage is going. More than that, each has learned to be more independent within the relationship and to stand alone a little better, by taking on some of the responsibilities that they would normally have left to the other.

Most of us dread losing our independence and having to accept help from others. It is hard to learn to do so in midlife, when we expect to be the ones giving help and support to others. Learning to receive as well as to give, with good humour and not too much fuss, can be an important step forward in personal maturity.

Changing course

As we've already seen, a common midlife symptom is a sense of restlessness and the desire to chuck everything up and start afresh. The most quoted example of this syndrome is the artist Gauguin, who followed a respectable career in banking until he was thirty-five, then left his wife, his job and later his country to follow his artist's bent. Within five or six years he had become a leading painter of the Post-Impressionist School.

A few years ago there was a trend to make a similar total change of life by opting out of the city rat-race in exchange for 'the good life' and a small country living.

Other people put in for early retirement in order to give ten or more years to a caring organization. The actor Brian Rix left the stage at the height of a highly successful career, in order to work full time for an organization for the mentally handicapped.

Most professional advisers discourage people from making drastic changes during the crisis of midlife but a change of direction, properly thought through and planned for, can be a great success. Plenty of us lack the courage needed to part with secure routine and a regular income, but those who do remind the rest of us that there is more to living than comfort and security.

Running your own business

Some people have always had ambitions to be their own boss or start their own business. Whatever form the dream takes, it can sometimes be turned into a reality. It is important that married partners are both prepared for whatever risks and hard work are involved in starting up a business and being self-employed.

A bank manager in a seaside town commented on the number of couples who ask him for loans in order to buy a hotel in that resort. Many discover after one or two years at the most that, far from making a success of the venture, they don't so much as break even and can't repay their loan, so they sink further into debt. Most have no training in hotel management and have not realistically costed the venture.

The years of unemployment and redundancy have resulted in the provision of information centres and training to help the self-employed. There are free advice centres for those planning to set up a small business. It is important to get all the help and advice you can beforehand. One article on starting your own business points out the obvious areas of getting the money, finding the premises and paying for the professional advice of an accountant and solicitor. It also suggests asking yourself these questions, among others:

- Will anyone buy my idea?
- Does anyone else offer the same goods or services locally?
- Would demand for my goods be seasonal or steady?
- What is the product's estimated life? Is it just a passing fad?
- Could I adapt the product or find an alternative if I had to?
- Can I repay the loan comfortably within the specified time?

Working from home

Men and women who work as craftsmen, consultants, artists or writers may use their own home as office or workshop. It is a great saving of time and money, but there can be disadvantages. It is important — particularly for a woman who is also running her home — to set office hours, whenever possible. Anyone who has no secretary — official or otherwise — to answer phone and doorbell, has to deal with what sometimes seems to be a constant stream of interruptions, mostly unconnected with the job. It may be hard to persuade friends, for whom being at home means being off-duty, that you are not available during working hours to attend good cause coffee mornings, or hold lengthy conversations on the phone. In practice, many of us who work at home make compromises. You can't always turn people from the door. I try to remind myself that Jesus, in his very busy life, met with constant interruptions, and accepted them as part of the day's plan. So I try to do the same.

Some people who work from home are tempted to work long hours. Survival may depend on producing a certain volume of work but it is not good policy to drive yourself too hard. Regular coffee and lunch breaks are provided at work, and often involve some socializing and a feeling of being off-duty. It isn't possible to create the same atmosphere at home but it is important to build in some breaks during the day. Since home is also the workplace, a holiday away from home becomes more important. It is almost impossible to ignore phone calls and the letters that continue to come through the letter-box, or to turn a blind eye to your desk, and enjoy a holiday at home.

Back to work

Some women who have not worked since their children were born may decide to go back to work. Some are already qualified but may need to top up with a refresher course, which can restore confidence as well as bringing them up to date. Others may take advantage of government schemes to do a course of training for the first time. It is important that women who have stayed at home should value themselves properly. Some who had little or no work experience before marriage compare themselves unfavourably with those who have qualifications on paper, or have been years at their job.

A woman of forty upwards, who has brought up several children and managed a household, has a great deal to offer when put alongside an eighteen or twenty-year-old with very little experience of people or life. The 'mature' woman is used to making practical decisions and has a range of skills. She has probably learned to be cook, nurse, teacher, chauffeur and general organizer and manager — often doing two or three of these jobs at the same time. She is used to handling people — including teenage children, elderly relatives, neighbours, and plumbers, electricians, builders, and a host of others — and can cope readily with a wide range of potential customers or clients. She is used to bringing order out of chaos and turning her hand to whatever needs to be done. She is also likely to be reliable and conscientious, taking responsibility as a matter of course. What she needs is a little help and advice to enable her to face interviews confidently, and to sell herself in the way that her qualities and qualifications deserve.

Nearly all women who have remained within the home for ten or fifteen years comment on how much they have lost confidence through lack of contact with the world of work. Some develop mild symptoms of agoraphobia and feel unsafe outside their own four walls. This kind of reaction is normal. If they are patient with themselves and are prepared to be brave and determined, they will be perfectly well able to go back to work. One woman, who had been off work for less than two years, commented, 'Having a baby changes you. You are more vulnerable and some of the self-assurance and easy confidence rubs off. I know I have that to overcome when I start work again.'

'What I always wanted to do!'

Some women at forty are still living with the dream of what they would have liked to do or be. In some cases it is not too late to realize the dream. In recent years many people have taken qualifying exams and gained degrees when they are in their seventies, disproving the old theory that it is harder to learn when you are older. A person at forty is more likely to be single-minded about study and has a wealth of experience of life and people to enlarge their understanding in many fields. There are colleges ready to take mature students on a part-time or full-time basis in most large towns. Maria went to a local polytechnic at a time when her two daughters were studying for school exams and gained a good general Arts degree. She was accepted by the young students and benefited enormously in terms of confidence and realized ambitions as well as increased enjoyment and knowledge. There are also opportunities to take courses from home (as with the Open University in Britain).

Some women who have brought up a family feel that they are suited to go into one of the caring professions or to train for a job using some of the practical skills they have developed in the home. They may apply for a course that is practical as well as academic. It is often good for the family to take a share in the chores and begin to be more responsible for themselves at this stage. Relatives, or neighbours and friends, are often willing to give back-up during the two or three years when it may be needed.

Voluntary work

Voluntary work is often suggested as an alternative for those unemployed, or as an outlet for housewives and others who have time on their hands. In all fairness, voluntary work is quite different from paid work, in other ways than the absence of a pay packet. A neighbour told me how she had applied to do voluntary work at a local hospice and was asked instead to come as a paid member of staff. She explained the difference that had made.

'The doctor and I talk to each other in a different way. She can give me orders, tell me exactly how she wants a job done and in return expect work done quickly and expertly. She can criticize me and comment in a way that she could not do to a volunteer. In the same way, I can be critical of the system and be honest with her, just because I'm not a volunteer. She can dismiss me if she objects.'

Those comments do not imply that volunteers are inefficient or unreliable but that the relationship is based on gratitude and mutual convenience, rather than on a business contract.

There is another reason why some women do not choose voluntary work. They realize that most voluntary organizations, like beggars, cannot be choosers. They are looking for a job partly as a means of restoring lost confidence and need the boost that will come from being selected in preference to other applicants. The pay is welcome not only as a useful addition to the kitty but as proof that someone considers them worth their wage. These people are also looking for the discipline and constraints of defined working hours.

Having made these distinctions, it is most important to emphasize the immense satisfaction that people gain from doing voluntary work. The needs are great too. The co-ordinator of all voluntary work in one town said that there is such a need for volunteers that she would be able to answer all the calls for help only if everyone who was free gave one hour's help a week.

Many people may not realize the great variety of voluntary work to be done in any community. It is possible to use any and every kind of skill. The local hospital alone provides a wide range of opportunities. There is hospital radio work, for those with skills as communicators, a need for volunteers to visit patients, arrange flowers, take round the newspaper and magazine trolley, or service the tea and coffee bar. One hospital volunteer co-ordinator told me about two women who came in regularly to wash all the vases on every ward in a large hospital.

In other areas healthy volunteers may dig gardens for the elderly, care for gardens or parks as part of a conservation scheme, or go on archaeological digs. Volunteer centres produce sheets which list agencies offering long-term volunteer work as well as short-term projects. Local churches are centres for voluntary work too, often running their own playgroup, mother and toddler group and day centre and lunches for the elderly. Samaritans and marriage guidance organizations may require volunteers suitable for training. Voluntary workers usually find that they receive far more than they give, in terms of personal satisfaction, new interests, fresh insights, and a larger outlook on life. One volunteer described her experience in helping at a second-hand 'charity' shop. Now that she is living alone, she thoroughly enjoys the chance to meet people.

'The same people come looking for bargains,' she told me, 'and we get to know each other. It's always fun undoing the parcels that are sent. Then those of us who help try to meet for coffee from time to time, as we are on duty at different times. I get enormous pleasure from discovering how much our day's takings are and knowing how well the money will be used.'

Some people use free time to set up a support or pressure group for a cause which is near to their heart. Those who have a child, a partner or parent suffering from some particular physical or mental disability could start a local group for those in the same situation. Local doctors, district nurses or social workers could recommend contacts. In some cases there will be a central, national body to advise. Members of such local groups can share problems and helpful suggestions, give mutual support and perhaps arrange fund-raising events. Those who have previously experienced the limitations of caring for an elderly or handicapped person, but are now free from responsibility, might be able to offer occasional time off to someone still coping, whose problems she would thoroughly understand.

Increased leisure gives a great opportunity to widen personal horizons. Most towns provide day and evening courses in a wide variety of subjects and it is possible to learn languages, discover something about ancient history or natural history, practise the skills of cake-icing or painting or almost anything else that holds appeal. Costs are small and there are usually special rates for the unemployed. All these ways of using new free time are also ways of meeting other people and becoming outward- rather than inward-looking.

What is work?
We began this section by looking at some definitions of work. It is certainly more than a conventional job or paid employment. Michael Moynagh goes further and sees in the biblical concept of work something that includes leisure activity too. He believes

that God works constantly in order to sustain and restore the universe that he created. Humankind, made in God's image, has been given the authority to 'creatively manage' the earth. This, Moynagh suggests, includes the mastery of all nature's laws and can include learning to play the guitar, or to master the rules and skills of football, as well as to solve the laws of mathematics or physics.

By this definition all who are purposefully engaged in mastering skills and caring and maintaining order for others are at work, whether or not they are on a pay roll or receive payment at the end of the day. Such a view of work opens up new possibilities both to those who still have jobs and those who, through no fault of their own, have been forced out of conventional work through unemployment or ill-health.

ACTION CHECKPOINTS

☐ Be ready to accept changes in the work scene.

☐ Rethink your definition of 'work'.

☐ Adapt to possible new roles at work and at home.

☐ Consider the great possibilities of voluntary work.

☐ Explore new interests and leisure pursuits.

☐ Take confidence in who you are, not what you do for a living. Apply the same criterion to others.

SECTION 7
PROFIT AND LOSS

17

DEALING WITH THE PAST

The Things People Say

'There are lots of things where we have to learn to say, "I should have loved to do that but I can put it aside — it's not appropriate now."'
Therapist

'When I realized I'd made the same mistake again, I just went away and cried. But it seemed as if God said to me, "Don't think about your wrongdoing, think about my forgiveness."'

'I really don't envy young people — all that gaucheness and uncertainty. I much prefer being the age I am.'

'If it's still possible for you to go and achieve your heart's desire — go and do it! But if not, shut up about it!'

'Real guilt hangs like a ball and chain round our ankles, and impedes our involvement now in the joy that life can offer, and as it ties us with unbreakable bonds to the past, so it spoils all happy expectations of the future.'
Roy Trevivian, *So You're Lonely*

Most of us who have reached midlife look with admiration and a twinge of envy at a lively and attractive bunch of twenty-year-olds. We recognize that the world belongs largely to the young. If we're lucky, we can look back nostalgically to happy days when we were that age too. But many of us wouldn't really want to be young again. We know that in the years since we were twenty we have gained insights, experience and a heightened awareness of life that we would not trade in for any of the advantages of putting the clock back. Being twenty would be fine, if we could combine it with all the benefits of experience. So we do recognize that growing towards middle age is not by any means all loss. There is a healthy amount of profit to be enjoyed and we need to capitalize on the assets rather than bemoaning the opportunities and advantages that are gone for ever.

Those were the days!

Most people who are nostalgic about the past look back on some particular period of their earlier life when they believe that they were really happy. Some recall the time when parents were alive and the family home gave security and a sense of belonging. Others remember the early days of a marriage or the busy years when the children were babies. For some, the high water mark is the period when their job or career was at its most stimulating or most secure. It seemed as if life was really worth living at that stage and everything seemed in tune. One friend in her mid-fifties looked back to the time when her three children were in their teens. She remembered her now quiet and orderly house being full of youngsters. That for her had been the golden age, in contrast with the empty present.

Happy memories are meant to be among the assets of getting older, but clinging to the past instead of being rooted in the present is not real living. However good the past may have been it is not the only kind of good to be experienced. There are new and unexpected areas of living to be explored and enjoyed in midlife which were not on option in the days that have gone. Only by letting go of the past is it possible to stretch out for what is available now, as well as what still lies ahead.

'If only. . . !'

Not everyone looks back on the past wearing rose-coloured spectacles. Many people see the years that have gone in a negative way. They believe that their whole life has been spoiled by mistakes that occurred years before. If they had only had the chances they were denied, or had not plunged into relationships they now regret, their present life would be different and better. There are many variations on the theme.

'If only I had had a different start in life!' — 'If only I had been allowed to do the job I wanted' — 'If only I had not married' or 'If only I *had* married.' Others may look back to some disastrous event — 'If only this or that had not happened!'

Perhaps nearly everyone reaching midlife has at least one 'if only' from the past that still threatens to poison the present. Some missed opportunities can still be bought up but there are other events which were so final that there is no way in which to change their effects. Nothing can blot out the memory of parental abuse or of cruelty within a marriage. Accident or illness may have resulted in death or permanent disability to the person concerned or to someone they love.

Professional counsellors and wise laymen would all give the good advice — sit down and let your grief come to the surface. Give yourself time and space to mourn your loss, whatever that loss may be — of a partner, a child, a parent, a career, of health or home. Then, when the loss has been recognized and taken fully on board, come to terms with the present. Get on with living life as it is now and begin to build positively towards the future.

This is good advice, but it requires courage and stoicism to put it into practice. Not all of us feel able to summon up such resources.

A close friend of mine had to cope with the death of her son, as the result of an accident which occurred when she was driving the family car. She was in hospital herself, while she recovered from injuries. Afterwards she told me, 'I knew that somehow, before I came out of hospital, I had to come to terms with what had happened. Insofar as I felt responsible, I had to let God forgive me and I had to forgive myself too.' It would be a big mistake to imply that this kind of reaction is easy or avoids any of the pain, or that it happens overnight. But it is a positive instead of a negative way of dealing with the past and opens up possibilities for new responses and understanding.

Our society fears pain and suffering. Most of us think of them as evils to be avoided at all costs. It is right that we should do everything in our power to reduce suffering of every kind, but it is also true that suffering holds great potential for human growth and maturity. It's my experience that God is able to use suffering to deepen and enrich life for the people concerned and for those whose lives are touched by them. It is not uncommon to hear someone say about a hard and painful experience, 'I would not have been without that.'

The past cannot be recalled or altered but when it is handed over to God it need not continue to destroy the present. God is ready to forgive our self-will, our blunders and the deliberate harm we have done to ourselves and to others. He can help us to find a positive way forward, learning from the past, but leaving its mistakes behind. Plenty of people have also discovered that seeming 'accidents' and temporary loss have brought an eventual harvest of good.

'If it hadn't been for him!'

A variation on the theme of lost opportunities and unforeseen tragedy is the tendency to pinpoint one person as the cause of all our past misfortune. Father, mother, brother or sister, husband or child, employer or friends of either sex may be seen as the villain of the piece, whose influence or action in the past has spoiled our lives. A wife may be tempted to think, and say — 'If it hadn't been for him I shouldn't be in this mess now.' A husband may be perceived as the one who took her away from the congenial place where she had lived, who gave her (or failed to give her) children. He may be blamed for his cruelty, unfaithfulness or expectations, which left her unable to follow her chosen career.

Often a husband, or a wife for that matter, may be genuinely responsible for preventing a partner from developing freely as a human being. Sometimes parents make demands or impose restrictions which prevent their children from becoming fully adult and able to pursue their own chosen lives. But before off-loading responsibility for an unfulfilled past and unhappy present upon any other human being, we must be honest with ourselves. Are we finding a scapegoat for our own lack of ability, lack of courage or sheer laziness?

Eric Berne, the American psychologist, describes this ploy in his book, *Games People Play*. 'If it hadn't been for him I should have been a concert pianist' begs the question of whether the many hurdles to success that lie in the path of such a profession could really have been jumped. Had the frustrated musician really the ability to achieve success, the physical stamina to fulfil demanding international tours, or the disposition to cope with performing in public and being in the limelight? A similar number of imponderables might apply to any of the other thwarted ambitions for which we make another person take the blame.

By the time we reach midlife we should stop playing games and we should take responsibility for being the way we are. Eric Berne suggests that the woman who says, 'If it hadn't been for him,' may unconsciously have chosen to marry him because he would give her the excuse she needed for avoiding the ambitions she feared she could not achieve. We need not be afraid of admitting to our weaknesses. We have learned by this time that we also have strengths. We may not have achieved what we once aimed to do or be, but we have other things to compensate. Those who gave up some of the rewards of work may have a family and all the enrichment which that brings.

Those who have not had children have achievements at work and opportunities for experiences that they would otherwise have missed. There are few ways of life so restrictive that they have no accompanying benefits and it is just as realistic and does us far more good to count up the credit instead of the debit column.

Sometimes it is still possible to achieve ambitions that had to be put aside in the past. Parents may not have allowed their children to go on with their studies or apply for the job they wanted to do. In midlife it may be possible to have a second chance. A man who was pushed into a secure job may take the risk of changing his career. Others, with relatively undemanding jobs, may deliberately accept a lower rung on the ladder. In this way they have the scope and energy to develop, outside work hours, the creative talents they once wanted to pursue full time. Plenty of writers and artists, past and present, have kept their bread and butter job in order to be free to write or paint without financial worries.

Sometimes it is worth exchanging a dream that cannot now be fulfilled for a reality which is possible. One friend, whose father would not let her nurse, works for the Red Cross as an instructor and first aid helper. It is healthier and more fulfilling to make compromises of this kind than to live with a continuing sense of regret, or to look for vicarious fulfilment through a son or daughter. For those who are not too proud to accept them, the consolation prizes in life can be very rewarding.

The way we were brought up

Sociologists may differ as to the relative importance of nature and nurture — heredity and environment — but how we were brought up has a lot to do with the kind of people we are now. Our values, our capacity for enjoyment and our self-esteem all depend on attitudes taught and demonstrated to us when we were young. Those who have had experiences of bad parenting or of broken family life may be damaged emotionally. Some regret the lack of positive guidelines in their upbringing but probably far more, who are now reaching midlife, resent an upbringing that was too strict and rigid. Some were brought up in homes with strong moral or religious codes and then found themselves, as late teenage students, adrift in the free permissive world of the swinging sixties. Some threw over the moral and sexual taboos they had grown up with, but were still deeply aware of the moral authority they had rebelled against.

Those who reacted against their received code of morals may suffer doubts and uncertainty in midlife.

Other people, who have continued over the years to toe the parental line, out of habit or from fear of opposing a forceful parent, may also have problems in midlife. They have retained a set of beliefs without ever having a faith of their own. This kind of second hand moral or religious structure will not help them cope with crises or difficult events of life.

But it is not so easy to discard what loved or powerful parents have taught without feeling guilty. Even when parents are dead, it may seem to be doing violence to their memory. But it is damaging in the long run to carry into adulthood a set of taboos and beliefs that have not been personally tested and made our own. The crunch often comes in midlife, when some event makes the whole flimsy structure of 'belief' collapse. However, the antidote to parental indoctrination is not scepticism but the search for a faith that is personal and rooted in reality. Such a journey into self-awareness and reappraisal in the midst of midlife crisis is difficult, and may require the help of an understanding friend, minister or other professional counsellor, but it is infinitely worthwhile.

Josie grew up in a happy home where the whole family went to church but without any narrow religious restrictions. They all enjoyed a wide range of cultural and leisure pursuits and the children accepted Christian standards as part of the loving family life. She found it relatively easy to come into a faith of her own and is having few problems in adapting to the changes that come as her children grow up and begin to go off to college. She is delighted to have a bit more time to take up interests she had shelved during the busy years.

George, her husband, grew up in a home dominated by a powerful father, where to criticize or to show anger was taboo. Unable to blame God or to criticize his parents, now dead, he has suffered instead from a deep and long-lasting depression, feeling himself utterly worthless and unfit to be loved.

Both Josie and George are equally the objects of God's love and care but, because of their different upbringing, Josie is free to enjoy that love and develop as a normal and mature woman while George is still finding it impossible to see either himself or God in a true light. His personal search for self-worth based on God's actual valuation is taking a long time and is very painful. He needs professional help and the support of his wife as he rejects what was false in the past and works his way towards healing and truth.

Anger and bitterness

Many people feel anger and bitterness about the past. Sometimes that anger is directed openly towards the person who seems to have spoiled their life through carelessness, selfishness or deliberate cruelty.

Doreen discovered that her husband was having an affair and took her revenge. She fought physically with the other woman as well as maliciously — and falsely — reporting her to the police for soliciting. Her husband returned to her but she told the marriage counsellor, 'This man has wasted thirty years of my life and I have got to get my revenge.' She did so and destroyed her husband, their marriage and her own peace and happiness.

More often, resentment and anger are kept under wraps. But they are still there. All professional counsellors agree that holding on to these negative emotions harms the person concerned more than the person they wish to hurt. In *Superwoman*, Shirley Conran advises: 'Don't hate anyone: it's a destructive waste of energy. Try to ignore that person and try to make sure that you are no longer vulnerable to him or her.' But ignoring someone with whom you live or work closely is not always a practical proposition. The Christian solution is to replace the hatred and anger with forgiveness and love. That is not a weak option, in fact it is a response which even the strongest person is unlikely to manage without God's help. God is love and is totally forgiving, so he can show us the way to forgive.

Barbara, now in midlife, remembers a childhood overshadowed by her father's overbearing behaviour towards her mother and all the family. Her mother died when Barbara was still a young woman. Her father comes over most Sundays to have dinner at her home. 'I have forgiven him,' Barbara said, 'and I can feel right about him while he's not there. But the moment he comes into the house and begins to behave in the same old way, I find it hard. I have to keep on forgiving him, over and over again.' C.S. Lewis suggested that when Jesus told us to forgive the person who wrongs us 'seventy times seven times', he means us to keep on forgiving the same specific wrong over and over again, when that's necessary.

Guilt

A psychiatrist, interviewed on radio, said that every patient she saw was suffering from feelings of guilt. Whatever the reason for feeling guilty, the fact remains that guilt which is not dealt with causes deep problems. Midlife is a time for dealing with the root cause. The reasons given for a sense of guilt vary from one school of psychology to another. Most believe that it is inextricably linked to the process of growing from an entirely self-centred human baby into a person who must give as well as take and abide by the rules governing family and social groups. Guilt is therefore a factor that needs to be understood rather than forgiven.

It is important to recognize that a *sense* of guilt is not necessarily an indicator of something that needs to be forgiven. There are plenty of people who have enormous guilt feelings about the food they eat or the way they do their housework. Betty Friedan quotes one young mother who said, 'Clean sheets twice a week are now possible. Last week, when my dryer broke down, the sheets didn't get changed for eight days. Everyone complained. We all felt dirty. I felt guilty. Isn't that silly?'

At some slimmers' clubs, members are encouraged to 'confess' when they have broken the rules and eaten 'bad' things. The whole business of slimming takes on moral overtones which it doesn't possess.

Adults who have had rigid and perfectionist parents may also suffer from extreme feelings of guilt about their personal behaviour. Not only religious families are to blame.

Terry was the daughter of good, convinced humanists and had been brought up to take her responsibilities to society very seriously. She was constantly anxious and guilty about the times when she had failed to do all that she could or should for others, whether it was appropriate for her to feel that way or not.

All the same, when we are being honest with ourselves, we know that as well as suffering from false guilt we have also said and done things in the past which we are right to feel guilty about. Roy Trevivian, in *So You're Lonely*, puts it like this: 'Is there anyone with nothing to hide? I doubt it. . . Everyone has their secret store of guilt and because of its existence everyone experiences a corresponding sense of loneliness. It is not by chance that at the heart of the Christian message Jesus called (and calls) for people everywhere to repent and accept forgiveness. It is obvious to me that Jesus knew that eating at the heart of every human being like a cancer lies a burden of guilt which can be healed by the word of forgiveness.

'At the heart of the Christian gospel is the cross. That cross is God's way of saying that if you are truly and honestly sorry for what you have done wrong, then forgiveness and freedom from guilt are yours. It puzzles me why so many people ignore ·this priceless gift.'

Barry talked about the difference that the 'priceless gift' of forgiveness had made to him.

'I'd lived a pretty rotten life. My past was a mess. I'd had a divorce and a couple of spells in prison. When God forgave me it took a while for me to let him clean the whole of my life up. It reminds me of what happened to some friends of mine. They took over an old, dilapidated mansion. They started off in the vestibule and put that right. Then they had to tackle each room, one by one, dealing with damp and dry rot and everything else that needed doing. It's been like that with me. I know God forgave me straight away, but the mess that I'd made of my life was still there. It seems to me as if I've just had to let God go through the house, as you might say, putting things right. I kept opening up a bit more of me — another room if you like — for him to clean up and put right. So the whole process of repairing and healing every area of the past has taken a few years.'

Healing of the past may take time. Pain is not removed by a magic wand. Some of the consequences of what was wrong will not be undone. But receiving forgiveness — from God and from those we have wronged — as well as forgiving those who seem to have spoiled our lives, is an important part of dealing with the unfinished business of the first half of life. It is only when we have dealt honestly and effectively with the past that we are ready to set out unencumbered and with high hopes on the second half of the journey.

ACTION CHECKPOINTS

☐ Stop blaming others for what went wrong.

☐ Fulfil any postponed ambitions, if that is possible.

☐ Come to terms with what can't be altered from the past.

☐ Do something about your guilt — ask for forgiveness.

☐ Forgive those who have wronged you.

18
THE WAY OUT OF THE WOOD

The Things People Say

'For all that has been — Thanks! To all that shall be — Yes!'
Dag Hammarskjöld

'We make our choices and they make us.'

'I wouldn't be young again for anything. I can be so much less inhibited now. I know how to cope with situations and don't feel embarrassed.'

'My assessment of how most people experience their forties is that they're the best years so far. It's much more a time when earlier problems have been come to terms with than one when crippling problems arise.'

'I think that contentment is the proper goal of the last chapter of our lives and that people who fall into it too early can solidify their own well-being and turn their backs on the suffering around them.'
Bishop Jim Thompson, *Half Way*

'A crisis is a significant turning point which causes consternation because it presents new problems to which there are no immediate answers.'
Dr Brice Pitt, *Making the Most of Middle Age*

'Depending on your point of view, the menopause and the twenty years that follow can be regarded as either a problem or a privilege.'
Dr Jean Coope, *Menopause*

'To refuse to grow old is as foolish as to refuse to leave behind one's childhood.'
Jung

*'It is no easy matter to accept that one is growing old, and no one
succeeds in doing it without first overcoming his spontaneous refusal.'*
Paul Tournier, *Learning to Grow Old*

*'In the ongoing flux of life, (the person) undergoes many changes. . .
every change involves a loss and a gain. . . in all these situations
the individual is faced with the need to give up one mode of life
and accept another.'*
Dr C. Murray Parkes, psychiatrist

I have been told that the Chinese word for crisis is repre-
sented by two initial letters standing for the words Danger and
Opportunity. Every turning point contains these two possible
ingredients and midlife crisis is no exception. Everyone who
arrives at this stage has to negotiate the passage to a satisfying
second half of life's journey and that crisis is bursting with
opportunities as well as being fraught with danger. Up to now,
this book may have highlighted the dangers that most people
fear or actually experience in a midlife crisis. But it is even more
important to recognize the opportunities. The way ahead is full
of new challenges and new satisfactions. Even the supposed
bogeys of middle age and old age only look threatening viewed
from one angle.

The way ahead
In her book, *Passages*, Gail Sheehy quotes the words of the
poet Dante, written when he was just past forty: 'In the middle
of the journey of our life, I came to myself within a dark wood
where the straight way was lost. Ah, how hard it is to tell of
that wood, savage and harsh and dense, the thought of which
renews my fears. So bitter it is that death is hardly more.' Dante
was writing in the fourteenth, not the twentieth century, but his
description of the dark wood may neatly sum up the way many
of us feel at midlife.

What matters now is to find our way out of the wood.
Discovering a way forward is not the automatic result of the
passing of time. We don't necessarily emerge from midlife with
a clear sense of direction and purpose. For a start we must be
prepared to go forward, then we must find our bearings.

New beginnings
Seizing the opportunities offered at midlife and beyond involves
being ready to adapt and to accept new challenges. In order

to do so we must be willing to lose some of the satisfactions that belong to youth in order to enjoy new and different kinds of satisfaction and achievement. We must be open to change, instead of digging in our heels and refusing to budge from the familiar track.

When she was fifty, Brigitte Bardot told reporters, 'It's really difficult growing old. People who say "It's marvellous to be fifty" must be mad! I've got the temperament of a young girl. I dance, I play the guitar, and I feel as if I'm fifteen, but my face doesn't fit. . . It's not only the end of youth that gets me. It's the beginning of all the problems with one's health — I who have never been ill. In another ten years? It will be worse. I'll be sixty and prefer not to think about that.'

'The beginning of all the problems' — 'In another ten years it will be worse' — 'I prefer not to think about it.' These words represent the attitude of those who choose to remain, forlorn and lost, in the dark wood. Daniel Levinson, a Yale psychologist, made an in-depth study of adults. He wrote: 'The most distressing fear in early adulthood is that there is no life after youth. Young adults often feel that to pass thirty is to be "over the hill". . . the middle years, they imagine, will bring triviality and meaningless comfort at best, stagnation and hopelessness at worst. Middle age is usually regarded as a vague interim period, defined primarily in negative terms. . . the connotations of youth are vitality, growth, mastery, the heroic, whereas old age connotes vulnerability, withering, ending, the brink of nothingness.'

If this is how younger people really perceive middle age and old age, it is not surprising that they feel no excitement or sense of adventure at the prospect of embarking on that next stage of life. J.P. McErlean, who lectured for the Pre-Retirement Association, wrote about the popular misconception that 'age is a falling off, a diminution, a disability. Literally, a dis-ability. No one actually says it aloud, but it is there, in the atmosphere.' He says, 'It is important that we should fight this false assessment of old age, especially in our own minds. For who would strive to get the utmost from any stage of life if convinced beforehand that it offered no prizes, no rewards?'

Some of the commonly held attitudes to middle age and old age are based on the false value judgements of the society in which we live. In order to look ahead with a sense of purpose and promise, we need to discard what is false, recreating the expectations of the second half of life in a truer way.

A new realism

Levinson uses the words 'growth' and 'mastery' to express young people's definition of youth. But these are words which more accurately define middle life. Certainly early adulthood is taken up with striving to master skills and stake out a career, but it is when the hectic earlier years of exhausting endeavour at home and at work are past that people have the time to consolidate their experiences of life and to make sense of them.

At midlife there is the opportunity to stand back and take a longer and more detached look at ourselves and our achievements. From this vantage point some so-called successes may seem unimportant, and failures may show up as occasions for growth. There can be a new understanding of what really matters in life.

Some people capitalize on these new insights and revise their way of life in order to become more rounded and complete people. They develop those aspects of themselves that were neglected in the rush to achieve and survive. Some major on their creative ability, full time or as a satisfying hobby. Others give more space and time to satisfy intellectual needs and to develop and deepen relationships. Those who arrive at middle age and old age with these insights are the most likely people to have achieved wholeness and rounded personal growth.

Someone described middle age as 'a period filled with rewards and challenges. There is a sense of being settled, of having found one's place in life, and of being freed from the demands and responsibilities of raising small children. When compared with younger adults, middle-aged people often have more financial security, positions of prestige and leadership in the community, more opportunity to travel and increased wisdom.'

A new kind of wisdom

Wisdom is often recognized as the hallmark of older people and in many societies the elderly are respected and revered for their wisdom. Sadly, in our society, technological advances and medical and scientific discoveries lead people to assume that new is better. In times when work methods changed very little from one generation to the next, words of wisdom and instruction from the old were listened to and followed. Now to be old is to be out of touch with new methods and advances, so it is tacitly assumed that old people are behind the times, and have nothing of value to contribute. But there are still many areas where the accumulated wisdom of older people is of great worth to the community. New is not automatically better in the world of the arts, of philosophy or in the field of relationships.

I discovered that the word for 'wisdom' used by the ancient Hebrews, means the ability to cope, in any and every area of life. When the Bible talks about having wisdom, that is what it means. It is also assumed that an ability to cope depends on a right attitude to God's guidelines and to his authority in our lives. One of the qualities of growing older is the increased ability to cope with all that life may bring. Others also benefit from that accumulated experience. But wisdom is not an automatic prize of age. We acquire it when we are willing to learn from our mistakes as well as our successes, and to understand ourselves as well as what makes other people tick. I, for one, am thankful that God promises to give wisdom generously to anyone who asks him for it. My own stock is still strictly limited.

A new kind of success

A negative attitude to middle age may also result from accepting society's definition of success. That word is associated with achieving goals in areas of physical looks and energies, status, money and fame. For people reaching midlife many of these goals are now out of reach. Some do come to middle age and old age with prestige, fame and money as assets. But those who don't — and that's most of us — are in danger of writing ourselves off as failures unless we redefine success.

If we look at life more realistically we recognize that success doesn't depend on these glittering prizes. We are aware that many who are outwardly successful are unhappy people who have failed to make enduring relationships or to find peace and purpose in life. True success has much more to do with using every opportunity and every ability to the full and learning to live with ourselves and with other people in a satisfying and liberating way. It means finding answers to some of the important questions about the purpose and meaning of life. This kind of success is more likely to reward those who have reached — and passed — midlife.

New identity

We have already suggested that in midlife we face a second identity crisis. Within the crisis lies the danger of losing our sense of personal worth, but there is also a golden opportunity to discover who we really are and what makes us of worth. In earlier years we may have taken our identity from the job we do. That will not usually last us for life. Or we may have borrowed our identity from another person — a parent, husband or children. But we are reaching an age when we can no longer expect to 'piggyback' our way, as Gail Sheehy describes it. We must discover who we are in ourselves.

Sadly, many people, stripped of props and labels, have a very low estimation of their own worth. Some of us are afraid to let ourselves — let alone others — see the person we really are. We need the esteem of others to bolster our poor self-image.

A doctor who is also a counsellor told me: 'People often try to help someone who is feeling a failure by suggesting all kinds of alternative fields in which they achieve. But that only shifts the burden without lifting it. They still believe that they have to achieve in order to be of some value. The truth is that we don't have to be or do anything in order to be of worth. To God we are infinitely precious and worthwhile, just because we are the unique beings that he has made us. He loves us and finds us infinitely worthwhile in ourselves. Knowing that brings a sense of freedom and purpose.'

The discovery that we are of intrinsic value makes it possible for us to stop pretending. It can be an enormous relief, by midlife, to discard the masks and be our true selves. We are probably not as 'grown-up' as we should like to be, for something of the child remains in all of us, which is often a good thing. If we know that God, who made us, loves us, we can be free to accept ourselves, warts and all, without pretending. We can also afford to let other people see the real person behind the discarded masks.

Acceptance

The word acceptance often has the ring of resignation about it — a kind of 'what can't be cured must be endured' philosophy. But to accept is not to suffer the inevitable but to hold out our hands to receive a gift, eagerly and thankfully. The key to facing the second half of life is to accept it with high hopes as a welcome gift. Because we now know more about life, we shall be realistic in our expectations.

Acceptance means rejecting the myth of total fulfilment. The cottage in the country, covered with roses, may never be mine, nor may sexual satisfaction, the perfect partner, wealth, children, or a number of other general or specific things that we feel sure would bring personal fulfilment. But then, no human being is likely to find total fulfilment. Looking at others, we are often unaware of what they have been denied, but they have their unfulfilled desires too. The secret is to enjoy and benefit from the things that we do have, rather than hanker in vain for what is beyond reach.

Acceptance means welcoming life as it really is. An Australian friend recently said, 'I used to keep thinking — "when this particular bad patch is over, everything will be fine." Now I realize that pain and suffering are integral parts of human life. They won't ever go away. They are just as much a normal ingredient of life as happiness.'

Centuries ago, someone described trouble and pain as positive rather than negative ingredients of life. His recommendation was, 'When trials come, welcome them as friends.' That may seem to us to be going too far. But we may have learned that we do grow through the hard and difficult experiences in life.

In a television programme about midlife, the presenter commented that those who accepted age were the ones who seemed to stay young. Paradoxically, those who are afraid of what lies ahead and cling vainly to the past, grow old. They still remain, unhappy and confused, in Dante's dark wood.

New goals

There is no magic formula to turn people at midlife into the kind of wise and self-aware people we have described. Everything depends on the kind of goals we set ourselves in early life and those we redefine at midlife too. Some people plan for material rewards and set out to find personal fulfilment and satisfaction. Shirley Conran advises women to be 'constructively selfish'. She urges people to 'ignore accusations of selfishness, egotism or ruthlessness from those who resent that you won't do what they (selfishly) meant you to do. The need for self-preservation forces everyone to be selfish.'

By contrast Jesus told his followers that those who deliberately lose their lives for his sake will gain life. To lose life can include foregoing personal comfort and purely selfish ambitions in the interests of an over-riding and greater ambition. These are the people that Jesus described as life's winners. This is not a philosophy of masochism. Plenty of people find happiness and fulfilment in caring for a partner, a parent or a child, in giving to society instead of considering their own needs. They are motivated by a love that is greater than self-love.

Jesus goes further and says that love for God comes first, even before love for others. The centre of the universe is not myself, not even the person I love more than myself, but God. Discovering his love for us and responding in love to him is not a mystical, airy-fairy experience, but a reality which forms the solid foundation for many people's lives and is the mainspring of their actions. Gladly saying 'I'll do what you want,' to God, makes love for others as well as love for ourselves possible. Everything falls into its right place.

New faith
The goals that we set for the second half of life will be closely related to what we believe and how far we have found answers to the age-old questions about life and death. Those who believe that life is an accident of evolution and ends at death have different goals from those who believe in a God who made us and cares personally about us. If I am answerable only to myself, I owe it to myself to find enjoyment and physical and emotional satisfactions as far as I can. If I believe that I belong to God and have to answer to him for what I do and am, the objectives in life will be different and other factors will carry weight. In *Half Way* Bishop Jim Thompson writes about the dimension that faith adds to life:

'While some may take refuge in religion and seek to use it as a crutch, many more have found faith and discovered a wholeness that enables them to walk tall and to be free. Faith is not a solution to life, it is a way of living it. Faith does not free us from perplexity, or even our share of agony, it rather affirms the meaning of our life and through the struggle gives us some assurance of God who is in the middle of all the mess. Faith does not bypass human destiny, it opens wider and offers us abundant life. Abundant life does not mean painless, anodyne life, it means life lived to the full, sharing its mysteries, its agony and its beauty.'

New hope
At midlife we face the challenge of looking towards middle age, old age and death. The prospect opens up new hopes of hitherto unexplored dimensions of life. One friend, still in her fifties, said, 'When you've begun to realize your own mortality, you are nearer to immortality and the idea of a God who is a creator and who is going to go on creating you. He knows the creatures he has made and is planning good for them. After this life he is going to use all our potentials and more — that were never used on earth. I used to think of heaven as being rather static and rather boring — sitting on

a cloud twanging a harp! — but it's dynamic. God will go on working on us.'

New love

At midlife, people need an overall purpose and goal that will take them out of the crisis and into middle age and which will be sufficient to last for the rest of life. When she was one hundred years old, Catherine Bramwell-Booth of the Salvation Army said, 'Someone who hasn't learned to love someone else better than themselves, hasn't learned to live. I have been rich in people to love.'

For some people, midlife represents a time when relationships are becoming fewer or poorer. Much-loved parents may now be dead, or children grown-up and away from close and loving contact. Marriage may be over. There is the option either of retreating into ourselves, unwilling to be vulnerable to further pain or sacrifice, or going out in trust to share love and care with others. Midlife and old age should not be times of impoverished relationships. We have the option instead to look outwards and to be rich in people to love. There are always opportunities for making new relationships. A woman of eighty-eight has recently made friends with her newly arrived neighbour, a young man of thirty. Both now gain enormously from their mutual friendship.

In *Who Walk Alone*, Margaret Evening describes her own moment of enlightenment, one cold winter's afternoon, as she sat by the fire, reading Elizabeth Goudge's novel, *The Dean's Watch*. The heroine, Mary Montague, was crippled as the result of a fall when she was a child. She decides at last to give up her fantasies of adventures she can never have, and her day-dreams of marriage and children, which will not come her way:

'With no prospects of a career or marriage it seemed that she was doomed to life-long boredom. But then in a moment of awakening, it dawned upon her that loving could be a vocation in itself, a life work. It could be a career, like marriage, or nursing, or going on stage. Loving could be an adventure. Quietly, she accepted the vocation and took a vow to love.'

Faith, hope and love are an ancient trilogy of virtues. They are also trustworthy companions to go with us out of the crisis of midlife into the new and exciting second journey which lies ahead. They will last us a lifetime, and beyond.

ACTION CHECKPOINTS

☐ Major on the assets of the second half of life.

☐ Rethink the ingredients of success.

☐ Be flexible — welcome new ideas and viewpoints.

☐ Look for some answers to questions of who you are and why you matter.

☐ Talk to some of the older people who have achieved wisdom and retain vitality — discover their secret!

☐ Make worthwhile goals to last your life.

BOOKS AND SOURCES

Material quoted in the text is used by kind permission of the copyright holders.

Dr Holly Atkinson, *Women and Fatigue*, Macmillan
Naim Attallah, *Women*, quoted from *The Times*, October 1987
Dr Eric Berne, *Games People Play*, Penguin Books
Shelagh Brown, *Drawing Near to the City*, Triangle
Myra Chave-Jones, *Coping With Depression*, Lion Publishing
Margaret Clarkson, *Single*, Kingsway
Elizabeth Collick, *Through Grief*, quoted from *The Times*, October 1987, Darton, Longman and Todd, in association with CRUSE (the Organization for the Widowed and their Children, headquarters at Cruse House, 126 Sheen Road, Richmond, Surrey, TW9 1UR, England). CRUSE provides help at national and local level, as well as leaflets and books on all needs concerned with bereavement.
Shirley Conran, *Superwoman*, Penguin Books
Dr Jean Coope, *The Menopause*, Martin Dunitz
Dr Richard Ecker, *The Stress Myth*, Lion Publishing
Margaret Evening, *Who Walk Alone*, Hodder & Stoughton
Celia Haddon, *The Limits of Sex*, Michael Joseph
Suzie Hayman, *Hysterectomy*, Sheldon Press
Professor Martin Herbert, *Living With Teenagers*, Basil Blackwell
Elizabeth Hodder, *The Step-Parents' Handbook*, Sphere Books, in connection with Stepfamily, the association set up by the author to provide support for stepfamilies, with headquarters at 162, Tenison Road, Cambridge, CB1 2DP, England.
C.S. Lewis, *A Grief Observed*, Faber Paperback
Sophia Loren, *Women and Beauty*, Century Arrow
Michael Moynagh, *Making Unemployment Work*, Lion Publishing
Malcolm Muggeridge, *Something Beautiful for God*, Collins
Dr Brice Pitt, *Making the Most of Middle Age*, Sheldon Press
Victoria Principal, *The Beauty Principal*, Hamlyn

Geoffrey Aquilina Ross, *How to Survive the Male Menopause*, Hamish Hamilton
Gail Sheehy, *Passages*, Bantam Books
Rose Shepherd, article on Marital Virginity, *Options*, September 1987
Lewis Smedes, *Sex in the Real World*, Lion Publishing
Dr Miriam Stoppard, *The Prime of Your Life*, Penguin Books
Bishop Jim Thompson, *Half Way*, Collins Fount
Dr Paul Tournier, *Learning to Grow Old*, SCM Press
Roy Trevivian, *So You're Lonely*, Collins Fount
Steve Turner, series of articles on Baby-boomers, *The Times*, 1986
Ann Warren, *Living With Unemployment*, Hodder & Stoughton
Dr Leslie Weatherhead, *Prescription for Anxiety*, Hodder & Stoughton
Dr John White, *Parents in Pain*, Inter-Varsity Press

Other sources

British Medical Association
Family Doctor publications on all aspects of health (catalogue obtainable from BMA House, Tavistock Square, London, WC1H 9JR).

Can a Carer Say 'No'. . . ? Report from the National Council for Carers, 29 Chilworth Mews, London W2 3RG, England. The NCC also provides a most helpful information pack and specialized booklets for carers, as well as offering help at national and local level.

Health Education Council
Booklets on diet, smoking, alcohol, etc. available from 78 New Oxford Street, London, WC1A 1AH.

INDEX

THE STRESS MYTH

Richard Ecker

* **Your boss is getting on your nerves**
* **Your children are driving you mad**
* **You've too much to fit into too little time**

Problems add up and the pressures of life get you down. This complex, uncertain, fast-paced world inevitably takes its toll.
  Right?
  Wrong.

This myth about stress, according to Dr Richard Ecker, is as incorrect as it is widespread. The battles of life do not have to make us casualties. Experts emphasize coping with stress, but prevention, says Richard Ecker, is the key. It begins with an accurate view of ourselves and of the world around us. Dr Ecker also helps us understand how unwanted stress affects us at home and at work, giving sound advice on how to find peace in the pressures of everyday life.

ISBN 0 7459 1269 9

COPING WITH DEPRESSION

Myra Chave-Jones

Depression is as universal as the common cold.
It may be little more than a passing mood. It may
be a dark shadow, robbing life of all joy. It may make
it impossible to carry out the simplest tasks. It may
last for only a short time, or drag on for months and
years.
What causes depression? How can we recognize it
in ourselves and in others? And what help is
available?
This is a helpful, practical, sympathetic book for all
who suffer from depression, and for those who live
close to them.

'A book for which many will be grateful.'
Dr Anne Townsend, *Church of England Newspaper*

'Sensible, sympathetic and positive.'
Church Times

ISBN 0 85648 360 5

A selection of top titles from LION PUBLISHING

FAMILY/PRACTICAL HELP

FACE TO FACE WITH CANCER Marion Stroud	£3.95 ☐
WHEN SOMEONE YOU LOVE IS DYING	
Ruth Kopp	£4.95 ☐
COPING WITH DEPRESSION	
Myra Chave-Jones	£1.95 ☐
THE STRESS MYTH Richard Ecker	£3.95 ☐
SIMPLE SIMON Ann Lovell	£1.50 ☐
ELIZABETH JOY Caroline Philps	£1.50 ☐
THE LONG ROAD HOME Wendy Green	£1.95 ☐
YOUR MARRIAGE Peg and Lee Rankin	£2.50 ☐
GETTING MARRIED IN CHURCH	
Mary Batchelor	£1.95 ☐
CHARNWOOD Grace Wyatt/Clive Langmead	£2.50 ☐
SEX AND THAT Michael Lawson/	
Dr David Skipp	£1.75 ☐
WILL MY RABBIT GO TO HEAVEN?	
Jeremie Hughes	£2.95 ☐
SINGLE PARENT Maggie Durran	£1.95 ☐

All Lion paperbacks are available from your local bookshop or newsagent, or can be ordered direct from the address below. Just tick the titles you want and fill in the form.

Name (Block letters) ....

Address ....

....

Write to Lion Publishing, Cash Sales Department, PO Box 11, Falmouth, Cornwall TR10 9EN, England.

Please enclose a cheque or postal order to the value of the cover price plus:

UK: 60p for the first book , 22p for the second book and 14p for each additional book ordered to a maximum charge of £1.75.

OVERSEAS: £1.25 for the first book plus 25p per copy for each additional book.

BFPO: 60p for the first book, 22p for the second book plus 14p per copy for the next seven books, thereafter 8p per book.

Lion Publishing reserves the right to show on covers and charge new retail prices which may differ from those previously advertised in the text or elsewhere, and to increase postal rates in accordance with the Post Office.